REVISED and EXPA

ELEVATING CO-TEACHING

with Universal Design for Learning

Elizabeth Stein

Foreword by Marilyn Friend

CAST | Until learning has no limits

© 2023 CAST, Inc. All rights reserved.

No part of this publication may be reproduced, stored in a retrieval system, or transmitted in any form or by any means, electronic, mechanical, photocopying, recording, or otherwise without the prior permission of the publisher.

ISBN (paperback) 978-1-930583-98-6
ISBN (ebook) 978-1-930583-99-3

Library of Congress Control Number: 2023932291

Cover and interior design by Happenstance Type-O-Rama

Published by CAST Professional Publishing, an imprint of CAST, Inc., Lynnfield, Massachusetts, USA

For information about special discounts for bulk purchases, please email *publishing@cast.org* or visit publishing.cast.org.

To all the variable learners who are committed to optimizing co-teaching and learning possibilities—that's YOU!

Contents

Foreword vii
Introduction: Embracing the Co-teaching Experience ix

PART 1   It Starts With YOU! Getting Grounded With Four Key Ideas

1   Key Idea #1: Embracing Context and Learner Variability. 3
2   Key Idea #2: Cultivating Expert Learners and a Growth Mindset. . 13
3   Key Idea #3: Exercising Flexibility as a Means of
    Addressing Variability 23
4   Key Idea #4: Applying Multiple Structures: A Review of
    Co-teaching Considerations and Six Models 37

PART 2   In the Classroom: Partnering With Your Co-teacher and Students

5   Getting to Know Our Students 61
6   Planning Powerful Instruction 71
7   Empowering Students as UDL Partners 95
8   Creative Structures: Making Space for Strategic Learning . . . 109
9   More Strategies and Structures to Promote Learner Expertise . . 121

PART 3   In the School: Partnering With Administrators, Community, and Caregivers

10 Elevating Partnerships With Administrators 157
11 Never Stop Elevating! Reflections and Next Steps 181
A   Appendix 189

References 209
Index 213
Acknowledgments 219

Foreword

When co-teaching emerged in the late 1980s as a means to ensure that students with disabilities were integrated into general education classrooms so that they could be educated with their peers and thus *included*, professionals—including me—focused primarily on the now well-known six co-teaching approaches, the co-teachers' relationship, and the dilemmas of arranging shared planning time and resolving issues such as scheduling. There was an assumption that if teachers were placed together in classrooms and given the opportunity to plan they would naturally develop lessons effective for all their students. As co-teaching evolved over the next three decades, it became increasingly clear that more was needed: The design, implementation, and evaluation of instructional strategies and techniques that empower all learners, is, after all, the real goal of co-teaching and one that cannot be accomplished by simply configuring students and teachers into a variety of groups. The second edition of *Elevating Co-teaching Through UDL* reflects Elizabeth Stein's deep conviction that employing UDL principles makes it possible to achieve the true potential of co-teaching.

Several aspects of this book are notable. First, terms that are often bandied about and sometimes treated as synonyms—for example, *inclusion*, *co-teaching*, *differentiated instruction*, and *UDL*—are clarified. This helps readers understand the nuances of and distinctions among these concepts and the application each has for planning and delivering their curriculum in inclusive schools. Commendably, Elizabeth avoids creating too-common dichotomies between terms (Is it UDL or differentiated instruction? Is it inclusion or co-teaching?), instead weaving all the relevant ideas into a rich tapestry that shows how all are crucial elements of contemporary education. Readers are encouraged to think about their own experiences so that they can recognize their current knowledge level, deepen it, and share it with colleagues.

Second, *Elevating Co-teaching With Universal Design for Learning, Revised and Expanded*, is written in a style that draws readers in. It uses a powerful voice combination of first person (e.g., *the first time I walked into the classroom where I was to co-teach . . .*), second person (e.g., *what would you do if . . .*), and third person (e.g., *teachers create a more accessible learning environment* . . .) that helps readers connect with Elizabeth, reflect on their current or future practices, and analyze critical points being made. I sincerely wish I could have visited a classroom where Elizabeth was co-teaching—I suspect it would have been an incredible experience to see her linking collegiality and masterful instruction!

Another unique dimension of this book is the attention to detail. Principles introduced in the early chapters are revisited and elaborated upon in later chapters as more content is added. Vignettes of what occurs as co-teachers meet, plan lessons, and share teaching are not just phrases or a couple of sentences; Elizabeth provides robust snapshots, often nearly a page in length, of what real teachers experience. By doing this, she illustrates the ways co-teachers can begin and refine their working relationships, negotiate partner challenges such as resistance to innovative ideas, interact effectively with their administrators, and demonstrate that students benefit immeasurably when their teachers collaborate. And through the summary at the end of each chapter and the insightful Study Group questions, readers can solidify their learning.

One additional example of attention to detail is the use of research and other citations from the professional literature. These are inserted just as they should be in a book that is so reader friendly—attribution is given when Elizabeth is directly quoting other authors or drawing on their work. The citations add credibility to the information outlined without detracting from its refreshingly informal style. To use a cooking metaphor, the references are just the right amount of seasoning, highlighting key ingredients but never overwhelming the main dish!

Elevating Co-teaching With Universal Design for Learning, Revised and Expanded, is a welcome contribution to school-based materials on co-teaching. It is an enlightening roadmap for teaching partners who are working diligently to keep their expectations high while taking into account all the different abilities their students bring to the classroom. It also provides administrators with essential understandings to guide them as they grow co-teaching in their schools and districts. Further, it is a book that could bring together college or university faculty members from various disciplines to explore how co-teaching could be integrated into all teacher candidate curricula. Most of all, this book is a beacon of the promise for all students when UDL is carefully embedded into co-teaching.

MARILYN FRIEND, Professor Emerita
University of North Carolina at Greensboro

Introduction:
Embracing the Co-teaching Experience

CO-TEACHING—meaningful and genuinely authentic co-teaching—is not a job for those who want to take the easy route. Since I began my co-teaching career more than 30 years ago, oh, the stories I could tell! My experiences range from the ideal to the extremely flawed. And I cherish each experience. My varied co-teaching opportunities served as valuable learning experiences that have shaped who I am as an educator. I have translated my experiences into a more developed mission with a magnified passion and deeper commitment to do whatever it takes to advocate for and with students.

Co-teaching is not always an easy position to be in—especially if one of the co-teachers is not on board with cooperation and collaboration. At the same time, co-teaching is one of the most rewarding experiences any teacher could have. There is always something to learn—and there is always more than one way of learning and teaching. Over the years, I have developed a co-teaching mantra: *Co-teaching is not a teaching assignment—co-teaching is a teaching experience.*

Every co-teaching experience is part of a learning process for all involved. When we allow ourselves to "go with the flow" and experience the ups and downs, along with the celebrations and the frustrations, we are open to embracing a solution-seeking mindset because we are immersed in experiencing co-teaching—come what may. When we experience co-teaching, we learn to take all situations in stride as part of a process as we keep the strengths and needs of our students clearly in sight. Our minds remain open and flexible, our thinking persists proactively and responsively, and our focus is set on our mission to provide the absolute best learning process for our students. And this focus is a stabilizing rock, so when we encounter those inevitable setbacks, that's just fine—they're just bumps in the road.

In the past two decades, Universal Design for Learning (UDL) has helped me put students first—no matter what my co-teaching situation happened to be—and to keep my vision clear through the process of designing instruction so that the strengths and needs of students remained a central concern. UDL allowed me to experience every co-teaching situation. UDL became my cushion to fall back on any time I needed to regroup and refocus on the most important factor: student connections and personal achievements. As my career shifted into a consultant, instructional coaching role, UDL once again became the structure, the language, and the oxygen that brought life to co-taught classrooms. When co-teachers relax into their co-teaching assignments, they are ready to learn something new, share their ideas, and work together to co-create learning environments that allow all learners (including the two teachers!) to experience learning as the meaningful process it should be.

In my first year of teaching in the early 1990s, I worked with two classroom aides, parents, speech and language teachers, occupational therapists, physical therapists, and behavior specialists. The class was composed of students with autism with a range of abilities. All of the educators worked together closely to give these students every opportunity to achieve at their absolute personal best. As the teacher, I needed to make decisions that affected everyone in the room. I included the opinions, talents, and ideas of all educators who worked closely with the students. Many of the students in the classroom did not speak with verbal language. We created communication boards (with laminated Velcro pictures—no computers back then!) and designed activities that provided opportunities for individual student voices. Students expressed themselves through pointing, dancing, smiling, nodding, or speaking. We, as a community of learners in our classroom, created an environment that allowed everyone to experience the concepts that we needed to teach.

Given to me by a parent, this original poster (all tattered and loved) expresses the essence of my UDL mindset that year (Figure I.1). I just didn't know it was UDL at the time! The classroom learning environment provided the opportunity for everyone in the room to experience learning in a risk-free, motivating environment. Each student had the opportunity to express their thoughts, feelings, and responses. Learning was not a chore or checklist of skills to learn and accomplish—it was an experience that created relationships with all educators and students, and with the learning process itself.

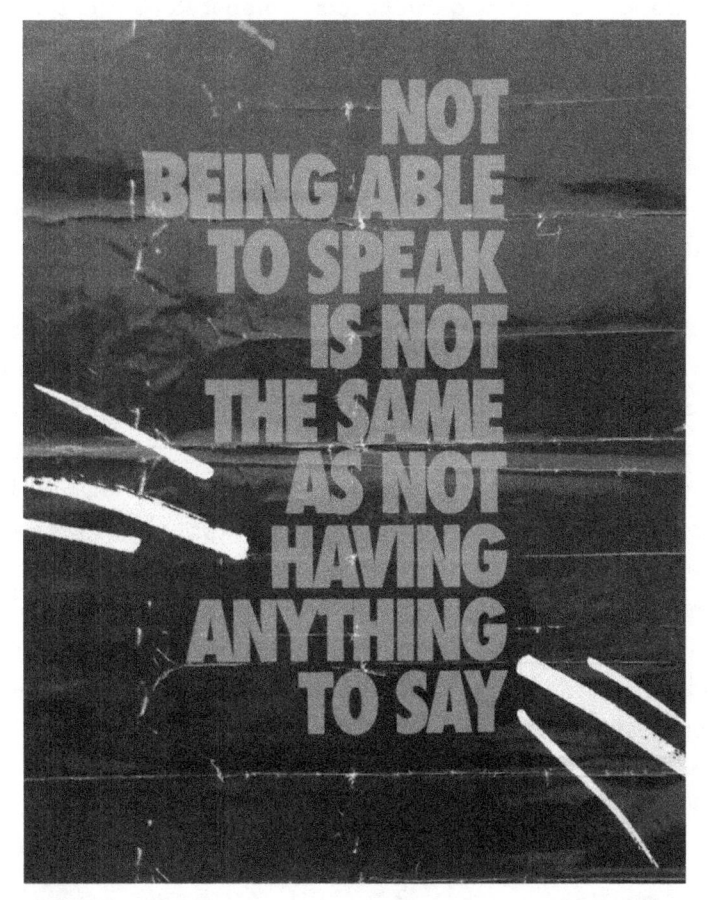

FIGURE I.1. Poster by Rosemary Crossley, educator and founder of DEAL Communication Centre, Melbourne, Australia. Created by the Division of Special Education and Rehabilitation, in Syracuse, New York.

As co-teachers, we must agree to join in a process of learning—both together as teachers and with our students as we pave the way for meaningful learning to unfold. Co-teaching can become so much more than just co-creating relationships and opportunities to experience learning. Imagine the ideal inclusive classroom setting where all students' thoughts are valued, all students' strengths are embraced, and all students' needs are met along a clear path that embraces individual strengths and allows learners to immerse themselves in the process of true learning.

My hope is that throughout this book, readers will have the opportunity to connect and to realize that this vision can come to fruition in their classrooms. Universal Design for Learning can become an educator's mindset that results in positive, meaningful learning environments for all students. In addition, students with disabilities, English language learners, and gifted and talented learners may feel empowered in general education settings when provided with the right opportunities for creating personal learning experiences, thus allowing them to make ongoing progress toward achieving their personal best. This book will provide strategies and action steps co-teachers can take to create successful learning environments for all students.

Two promises are held within the pages of this book. The first is to inform you, the reader, about the power that a UDL approach can have on any learning environment. This approach provides organically equitable learning experiences because the perspective of every learner is honored while guided by the teachers. The second is that a deeper understanding of UDL will ignite your connections, transform your thinking, and activate your ideas for specific ways to elevate instruction to meet the variable learners in your classroom. Any given well-intentioned and well-designed lesson will likely not be accessible to every learner in our classrooms. UDL provides the framework to ensure we can meet the broad range of abilities that gather there. The UDL framework becomes the bridge for creating meaningful access between where each student is and the content being taught.

Yes, I know—those are big promises to fulfill. But UDL offers a means to fulfill them. Just keep an open mind to the possibilities.

WHO THIS BOOK IS FOR AND WHAT IT PROVIDES

Preservice and novice teachers will gain the background to be knowledgeable while being inspired to adopt and implement a UDL mindset in their future classrooms. Veteran teachers, university professors, and administrators will begin to naturally connect to what they already know as well as learn new ideas and tools to instill a passion for learning within a barrier-free environment. This book is for new and veteran teachers who are ready to hit the ground running in UDL style. It is also a book for college professors and supervisors to use as they share the knowledge and necessity for student teachers to understand how to proactively plan and differentiate their lessons with precision to meet the diverse needs of students in inclusive settings.

This book will provide a foundation in key UDL ideas that need to be considered before we dive into practical strategies and routines to elevate co-teaching in any inclusive classroom setting. In basic terms, UDL is a framework of principles and guidelines for designing curriculum and instruction that connects learners with the learning process in meaningful ways. To put it another way, UDL is a method of thinking that proactively anticipates and plans for the needs of diverse individuals. This book serves as a foundation of knowledge, a launching point for implementation, and a sustainable guide for educators who want to ensure effective co-teaching and collaboration in their schools over time. Furthermore, this book invites educators to explore and expand their mindsets and their philosophical beliefs about how children learn. Educators must have a firm and flexible grasp of the ways they think about the learning process as a necessary part of creating a clear path between students of all ability levels, the content, and their relationship with learning itself. Teachers must think about what it is they have to teach and connect it with the strengths and needs of the learners in their room. These chapters discuss practical options for accomplishing this.

This book shares tips and strategies that can be used in classrooms right away. In fact, I steer away from technical research, definitions, and descriptions and dive right into the practical applications. This is a book for educators who want to engage their students in meaningful learning within the moments of class and far beyond. This is a book for teachers who have the privilege of working with a co-teacher and want to find ways to maximize each other's expertise, knowledge, and talents. It's a book for all those educators who continually ask themselves, "What can I do for children?" and who continually stay focused on their journey to find ways to do it. UDL has been the way for me—and I am so honored to be sharing my passion with you. There's something here for everyone!

WHAT'S NEW IN THE SECOND EDITION

This edition offers a new structure, additional strategies, updated research, and fine-tuned language across the entire text to explain key ideas about how UDL and collaboration serve as a solid path toward connecting with the diverse learners in our classrooms. Since I wrote the first edition, my own understanding of UDL has continued to expand as a result of my own research, doctoral studies, reading, reflecting, teaching in classrooms, and being invited to collaborate with diverse groups of educators in real classrooms across the nation. Here are some of the new insights:

- Let's start with the obvious: the title! The change from *Elevating Co-teaching Through UDL* to *Elevating Co-teaching With Universal Design for Learning, Revised and Expanded*, acknowledges my own learning journey since writing the first edition. Through my research, classroom experiences, and collaborations with readers of the first edition, I was able to expand upon ways for educators to initiate, sustain, and strengthen collaborative, equitable, and meaningful teaching and learning experiences.

- The second edition explores new and practical applications for today's classrooms. This new edition now structures the text into three parts that takes a "being grounded and branching out" approach:
  - Part 1: It Starts With YOU! Getting Grounded With Four Key Ideas
  - Part 2: In the Classroom: Partnering With Your Co-teacher and Students
  - Part 3: In the School: Partnering With Administrators, Community, and Caregivers

- This edition illustrates how UDL serves as a strong foundation for creating equitable learning by reframing how we view students with disabilities. For example, the importance of equity and inclusion is naturally embedded as readers further embrace viewing learners through the notion of variability rather than through a deficit-model lens. UDL becomes a strong lens that dismantles normalizing practices that may wrongfully classify students into disability categories.

- This edition provides revised explanations, language, and ideas. For example, an updated explanation of differentiated instruction and UDL is included as well as specially designed instruction (SDI) and updated classroom strategies.

- We now have an expanded view of co-teaching considerations—including how to select the most effective model with specific lessons.

- Study Group questions and Key Takeaways have been updated.

- New specific strategies are shared for strengthening administrators as active participants with any co-teaching team. The research-based strategies include my own research and practical applications in real classrooms across the United States.

- Additional "Co-teaching Connection" sections in Part 2 provide activities to strengthen your co-teaching relationship as you learn together along the year.

- A planning pages approach is shared to guide effective co-planning. This template is an at-a-glance, time-saving process that may make co-planning sustainable and meaningful—it has worked for me for over 30 years—across many co-teaching partnerships, and I am so happy to share it in this edition.

- Specific strategies are shared for sustaining strong partnerships between administrators and co-teachers.

This second edition structures the chapters into three parts to guide the reader along a natural process of individual, classroom, and school/community applications. Part 1 (Chapters 1–4) offers a foundation of important ideas. Part 2 (Chapters 5–9) introduces teachers to a workshop view as they begin to think about how to meaningfully connect to, reflect on, and apply UDL to elevate instruction in their co-taught classrooms. Part 3 (Chapters 10 and 11) extends the co-teaching partnerships to administrators, parents, and the students we are talking about throughout this book.

So be prepared to experience a potentially powerful mindset shift—it's all up to you! Let's begin by considering what it takes to create learning environments for students in co-taught classrooms. Allow your thinking to go deeper as you begin to look through a UDL lens; it's quite natural as you allow yourself to relax into the learning. Let's begin by focusing inward on our understanding of some key ideas. Let our co-teaching with UDL journey begin . . .

PART 1

It Starts With YOU! Getting Grounded With Four Key Ideas

Key Idea #1:
Embracing Context and Learner Variability

IT'S NO SECRET that learners with diverse and variable strengths, needs, backgrounds, and experiences are found in every classroom, right? Differentiating instruction to meet the needs of our diverse students is common practice—and just common sense. So why are so many classroom teachers still scrambling to close students' personal learning gaps? It's easy to blame the gaps solely on a lack of sufficient time and resources—or an emphasis on high-stakes tests at the expense of deep content work. But if we notice, observe, connect with, and focus on the students in front of us, there is so much potential for meaningful learning to take place. Traditionally, teachers have been differentiating instruction whenever possible. We provide additional supports for students who need it, but all too often students (far too many students!) fall out of our reach. We are left with thoughts of *How will I reach these students? Why isn't this student trying harder? What else can be done to help this student?*

Well-intentioned teachers plan their instruction based on what they believe a typical student in that grade level should be able to do. This traditional approach of planning for the so-called average student actually leaves many learners out. Teachers think they can pick up the pieces by providing extra help in hopes of supporting those students who are struggling. In addition, they may hope that the students who need more of a challenge will be inspired to pursue it on their own time. But why not create relevant, supportive, and challenging instruction within the moments of your class time?

In this book, we will turn our focus to designing curriculum and daily lessons in ways that support learners in real time—during instruction each day.

Let's consider a co-taught classroom—any classroom, with any two teachers. These teachers work hard to individualize the material to match students' specific needs. They soon find out this is a daunting task given the focus of the curriculum, the range of various learner needs, and the limited resources they have available. During the process of their efforts, some students' needs are met. But with all due respect for the teachers' efforts, too many students (typically those who struggle the most) are just not learning.

When these teachers begin to proactively plan by looking at the curriculum through a UDL lens (more on that in subsequent chapters), they are able to predict specific points in the lessons and unit where barriers to learning exist. They will understand the gaps between students' needs and the content and process of learning itself. A whole new world is open for teachers and their students when instruction is proactively planned for systematic learner variability rather than trying to support the needs of individual learners. We'll talk more about how to proactively plan this way in later chapters. But before doing so, it's important to understand and embrace the idea of individual variability.

SO, WHAT EXACTLY IS LEARNER VARIABILITY?

Consider this: Would you offer the same textbook to a high school senior as you would to a fifth or sixth grader? Ridiculous! Of course not! This is because we already have this idea of systematic variability. We know that developmentally these students require different learning experiences based on their age.

We understand this known systematic variability as *development*. We accept the process of monitoring the developmental milestones of infants, toddlers, and school-aged children through this linear view to make sure they are within the range of healthy development. We hear children referred to as "late" or "early" walkers or talkers because of the age they began to demonstrate that skill. We accept that children may achieve these milestones not all at the same time but within a range of time. We also accept that some students, due to disabilities, environment, or other factors, may achieve these skills outside of the typical range—or perhaps never at all.

In so many cases (and the faces of many students come to mind here), learners who fall short of what is viewed as average begin to believe that they are not as smart, as capable, or even as good as their peers. Parents, teachers, the students themselves, and society as a whole place a strong self-fulfilling prophecy on these learners, who then fall into the trap of not believing in the unique capabilities they possess that could indeed guide them to reach levels of personal success. Thankfully, research and neuroscience have revealed the significance of yet another layer of systematic variability that is evident in any learning environment regardless of the age of the learners.

The research of Kurt Fischer (1980), the late founder of Harvard University's Mind, Brain, and Education program, shows that an individual's skills are constructed over time with the idea of variability as the true "normal." Fischer stated that development is not a linear lockstep process that connects each step with the perfect achievement of new skills. Rather, development is like a spider's web—with growth and change occurring through many different pathways at the same time. Not only is there variability within skill sets, but learners demonstrate specific skills in specific contexts and not in others. Moreover, time is needed to allow a new skill or concept to progress. Therefore, it is typical for a student who is learning a new skill to regress or forget what they learned a number of times before the new skill can be a part of their repertoire of capabilities.

DYNAMIC SKILL THEORY AND THE CONTEXT OF LEARNING

Fischer's dynamic skill theory (Fischer, 1980; Fischer & Bidell, 2006) explains how an individual gains a specific skill set in relationship with their surroundings. Skills and behaviors are not things that a person has but rather a result of a person's interactions with their context (Rose et al., 2013).

Let's consider the implications for educators. Embracing context is critical! A co-teacher performs differently depending on multiple factors working together: the willingness of the co-teaching partner, classroom management practices embraced by their co-teacher, personal experiences with subject and grade levels, and the teacher's current skill level, to name a few—not to mention the physical temperature and lighting in the classroom. That same co-teacher may work with another co-teacher the next period, and their actions will be completely different depending on the new set of contextual factors.

The immediate context shapes the act of co-teaching and learning. This dynamic systems approach believes that the behavior of an individual—in my example, the co-teacher—is actively structured and context-dependent. Individuals demonstrate patterns of variability over time and in the moment-to-moment actions due to their interactions with their environment (Rose et al., 2013).

We can now begin to view learners through the lens of systematic variability, which highlights current brain research in support of neurodiversity and the fact that each brain is unique. Learners have a variety of strengths and needs that must be valued and nurtured in order for the individual to experience personal successes. Learner variability explains why each year we have similar experiences with students. The faces of students change, yet we seem to have similar concerns and celebrations in reference to student learning. In addition, learner variability explains why, year after year, teachers seem to be on a quest for strategies to motivate and engage the learners in their room. We hear similar gripes: "If only he would just apply himself"; "If only she would just do her homework"; "I don't know why he failed the math test, he was so attentive in class, and he came for extra help." And here's a classic: "I always get the same students raising their hands." Another common comment is, "She has a difficult home life with no support, so there's only so much I can do." But we must begin to take a deeper look into other factors.

Brain research supports the value that the emotions play a huge role in setting the stage for learning. Brain research also supports our knowledge that we can predict the ways that all learners will be different (Meyer et al., 2014). We can begin to proactively plan for the variability in our classrooms as we think about upcoming lessons. And these differences are highly variable and highly acceptable from a strengths-based view rather than a weakening deficit view.

This makes complete sense. Did you ever notice that year after year you have similar tales of woe when planning and implementing instruction? There are always those students who need more processing time. There are always those students who love to participate and express their ideas and have their hand raised every chance they get. There are always those students who avoid a task and seem aloof (or even defiant). And there are always those students about whom we say, "I don't know what else I can do—but I need to do something."

Year after year, we strive to engage our students in the learning experiences we create. And year after year, we have similar experiences with the types of learners in our classroom (with the exception of highly individualized experiences). With this view of learner variability, we now know why. We are all different in the way we perceive, engage, and express our understandings. This is even true of adult learning—think about your last experience in a class or workshop. Learner variability exists anywhere people come together to learn.

This is an extraordinary breakthrough for educators. It's a tremendously powerful view of designing learning experiences as we strive to guide learners to connect to learning. This is not something new or something additional for teachers to do. It is something that will serve to answer all our questions about what we can do to reach *each* learner in our classroom. Figure 1.1 shares the essence of understanding the link between the UDL principles and the notion of learner variability.

Action and Expression
- Learners vary in the way they process and express their understanding of information.

Engagement
- Learners vary in the way they engage with information.

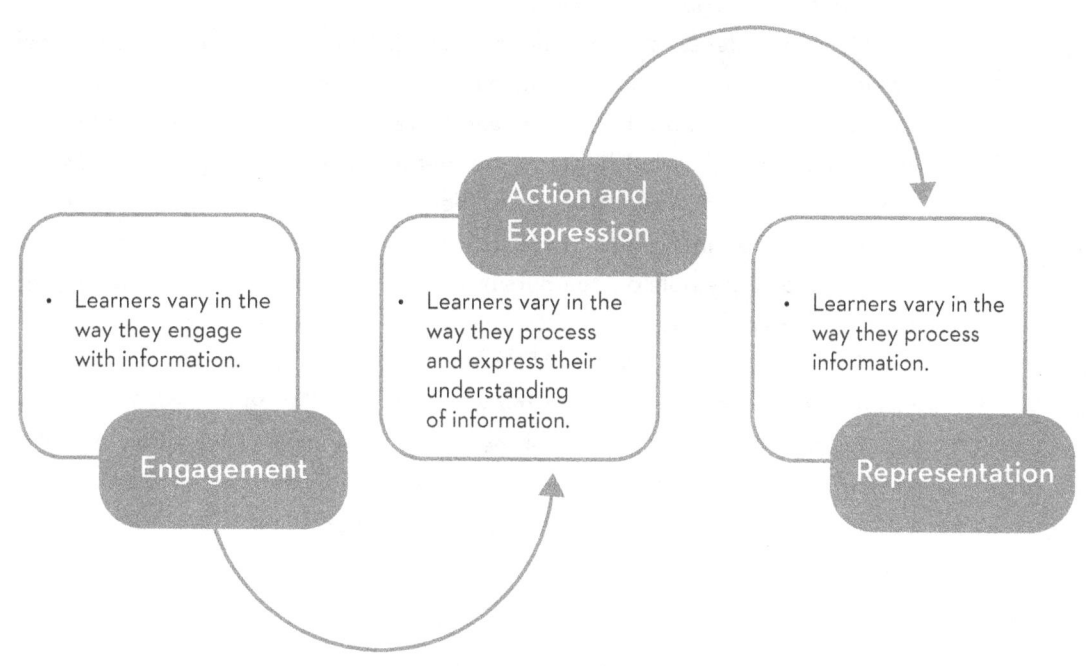

Representation
- Learners vary in the way they process information.

FIGURE 1.1. UDL principles and learner variability

All classrooms have variable learners, but inclusive, co-taught classrooms reveal additional value to proactively plan for variability. Through this variable lens, students will not be viewed by a label or category of disability. Rather, they will blend naturally with their peers in ways that welcome individual strengths and needs. Students will connect to learning in actual moments of instruction because their variability is a part of the classroom community.

Learning is a natural and accessible process because the teachers have a UDL mindset that illuminates students' engagement, understanding, expression, and ultimately their progress and achievements.

As mentioned earlier in this chapter, knowledge of learner variability has additional value in a co-taught, inclusive setting. In any given classroom, teachers experience a great range of students' abilities each year. Co-taught inclusive settings reveal an even wider range of abilities. The opportunity to have two teachers in the room to notice and address the various needs must be maximized by using co-teaching models (see Chapter 4) as well as applying each teacher's expertise. In addition, incorporating a UDL mindset can answer the question of how to reach such diverse learners by applying UDL principles and guidelines—more on this throughout the book.

Viewing students as variable learners breaks down many academic and social barriers resulting from categorizing learners into unnecessary groups based on learning deficits. With the belief in learner variability, teachers no longer view learners as struggling but begin to see that it is the very design of the lesson, the curriculum, and/or the structure of the environment that is the source of the struggling. Through the lens of variability, teachers can design learning experiences that do not single out learners by creating a class within a class but rather enable a flow of flexible group, individual, and whole-class learning opportunities.

Co-teachers who understand learner variability will not get into a routine in which one teacher is teaching the whole class while the other is pulling the "struggling" learners to the back of the room. Rather, they will carefully consider the instructional structures, strategies, roles, and relationships they create and thereby set the stage for all learners to achieve their personal best and become expert learners.

BREAKING THROUGH THE DEFICIT-MODEL BARRIER

Our current view of students with disabilities does not help our mission to value and educate all learners. In fact, this current view is undoubtedly one strong barrier in creating inclusive settings. To qualify for special education, students' strengths and needs are evaluated and their performance is assessed along an all-too-familiar curve where we can see how close to the "average range" they fall. If the students' standard scores place them between 85 and 115, they are identified as performing within the average range. The closer students are to 100, the stronger the perception that they are average learners. Students who perform below the range of accepted norms are considered to exhibit weaknesses that may need to be addressed through special education services. If students qualify for special education, they must meet the criteria for eligibility for one of the 13 categories of special education as defined by the Individuals with Disabilities Education Act (IDEA):

Autism	Orthopedic Impairment
Blindness	Other Health Impaired
Deafness	Specific Learning Disability
Emotional Disturbance	Speech or Language Impairment
Hearing Impairment	Traumatic Brain Injury
Intellectual Disability	Visual Impairment
Multiple Disabilities	

Our current system of special education encourages us to view students' abilities through this deficit model. We focus on what students are able to do with a zoom lens pointing to what they cannot do as compared to their typically developing peers. As students are compared to their same-aged peers, their weaknesses become the focal point. We decide what educational placements, programs, and strategies need to be in place to support individual students' areas of weakness.

This deficit lens predisposes students to the cloud of being negatively labeled as a student with a disability. This cloud accentuates what they cannot do—and what we, as educators, must do to help them. The way our educational system and society view these classifications far too often creates a barrier to learning. Learners easily develop a narrow view of themselves as learners simply by absorbing the messages (both direct and indirect) that parents, educators, and community members share. This deficit model becomes a way of thinking that focuses on the student's *disability* rather than the student's *abilities*.

However, when we as educators view learners through a variability lens, we consider all students as having a continuum of abilities and areas in need of improvement. As David Rose, lead architect of the UDL model, says, "Context is everything" (Meyer et al., 2014). To illustrate this, David points out that in situations where acute hearing skills are required, those with low vision or blindness may be more "abled"—they may have an advantage over their peers who have stronger visual skills and therefore rely less on listening. Learners on the autism spectrum often exhibit tremendous skills in situations that do not require social interaction or communication; their disability is largely measured by the context around them. Language differences, disabilities, gifts and talents—these all can shape the ways in which students interact with their learning environments and with the context around them. Accepting learner variability means considering students' strengths proactively in ways that positively address learning needs—leveraging rather than working around individual differences—and by doing so, helping guide learners to reach their absolute personal best.

Since writing the first edition of this book, I have realized there is a common misconception that Universal Design for Learning is often understood as synonymous with special education. Let's be clear: UDL addresses the needs of all learners (hence the word *universal*) along the continuum of what we know as general and special education. We must intentionally avoid that binary view. Remember, learner variability is everywhere learners gather; therefore, UDL serves all learners. UDL is a whole-school approach that includes learners with varying abilities, cultural backgrounds, and a rich range of diversity. As we'll see in later chapters, the framework benefits all learners through intentional yet organic design and implementation. UDL paves the way for additional instructional supports to unfold as needed. It can be the spark of light in any dark classroom. It provides a structured approach to planning, implementing, and experiencing learning, yet it illuminates all the spaces in between the structure that make way for co-teachers' flexibility and shared creativity with one another—and with their students. One example of creative structure is in the way co-teachers think about their students with and without disabilities.

Making the shift from a deficit mindset to a UDL mindset will open a world of learning to students and educators. As you read this book, you will continue to gain the knowledge, insights, and skills needed to adopt this mindset and overcome attitudinal barriers created by viewing learners through their deficits. With UDL, I know I am doing what is in each student's best interest, with the hope of creating students who understand how their personal learning strengths can become the access point for successful learning. The idea is for educators to instill the knowledge and experiences of a meaningful process of learning, not just have learners experience the "assign and assess" mode where the only thing they remember is a grade, a product, or some meaningless end result.

As inclusive settings become a natural part of the options for educating students with disabilities, we must make sure that special education teachers advocate well for their expertise as strategic, process-oriented educators. A special education teacher's training includes setting goals, monitoring goals, and scaffolding support to guide students toward independence. As standards-based expectations rise for all students, special education teachers must make sure to insert strategic supports within the moments of the general education instructional setting.

KEY TAKEAWAYS

✔ Research supports that we can predict the ways all learners will differ. Therefore, we can proactively design lessons for the natural variability that exists wherever learners gather.

✔ Deficit-model thinking can perpetuate viewing a student's weakness as a negative, as the focus is on what the student is not able to do.

✔ Shifting from a deficit model to a UDL mindset means we embrace all learners as variable. Students with a classification of a disability are a part of that natural variability.

✔ Variability encourages a strengths-based lens when viewing learners. A UDL mindset includes embracing an individual's strengths while working on areas in need of improvement.

STUDY GROUP QUESTIONS

1. Why is a teacher's view of students with disabilities so important?

2. How can the notion of learner variability empower teachers to empower their students?

3. Discuss your own learning strengths and areas of perceived weakness. Where do you fit along the notion of learner variability?

4. Who are your students? What are their strengths and areas in need of improvement? Select one to five students and discuss how they align with the idea of learner variability.

2

Key Idea #2:
Cultivating Expert Learners and a Growth Mindset

IF WE CAN AGREE that diverse and varied learners have the right and capability to meet high expectations, then we know that our curriculum needs to be flexible enough to make such learning possible. The burden of being flexible and accessible should be carried by the curriculum, not the learner, since the one constant among human beings is that they're different. But before we look at *how* to make the curriculum flexible (with UDL), let's think first about what we want to help our learners accomplish in the classroom. We will have content standards to meet for sure, as determined from state to state, district to district.

However, UDL is also premised on a bigger, broader goal: to help each person develop expertise in learning itself. This concept, incidentally, applies to students and teachers alike, since we are all growing toward expertise. The word *expertise* brings to mind a sense of mastery, suggesting that experts have achieved a high-level mastery of knowledge and skills. Yet, as we open up our minds to a deeper sense of what this concept really means, we see learning as a process with a series of valleys and peaks—times when we struggle and times when we reach mastery of our learning targets. Learning is about the behaviors and the attitudes needed to personally connect in a meaningful process that fosters a desire to keep learning. Learners are immersed in creating and following the action steps that lead to a desired outcome.

CULTIVATING EXPERT LEARNERS

This desire to be immersed in the process is what defines expert learners. Learning is not an end result. It is all about the process and desire to keep learning. The process itself is motivating—the grade or end product is not the sole source of satisfaction. The drive to learn is not about reaching the end result alone; the product or outcome is meaningful only when the process provides opportunities for each learner to connect and push through any obstacles or struggles in order to reach a learning target. The process is what provides the learners with the knowledge and skills they need in order to learn anything, anytime—and every time.

According to Ertmer and Newby (1996) the process of learning is a critical ingredient in the development of expert learners. Expert learners approach tasks with "confidence, planfulness, control, and reflection" (p. 1). Furthermore, expert learners are "strategic, self-regulated, and reflective" learners (p. 2). Since writing the first edition, I have embraced expert learners as learners who are on a continuum of performance on any given day. Keeping the idea of context and variability in mind, expert learners do not experience a step-by-step act of achieving skills and goals. Rather, they fall along a continuum that reveals their personal best in any given situation. Take, for example, eighth-grade student Gracie. She comes to school after not having had a good night's sleep. She has to skip breakfast, and she listens to her friend complain about her brother during the entire bus ride to school. Gracie now sits quietly during her first-period class. She is disheartened to realize that not only did she leave her homework at home, but due to an upsetting situation happening at home, she also forgot all about the math test now sitting on her desk. As she is completing the test, the sun glares through the window shades, irritating her eyes and causing a headache that's beginning to get worse from the mounting factors leading up to that moment. The next day in class, her co-teachers return the test. She failed. One of her co-teachers, Ms. McNally, approaches Gracie to find out what happened, saying, "This just isn't like you." Gracie replies, "I don't know, I just wasn't myself." Ms. McNally responds, "Would you like to take the make-up test on Wednesday?" Gracie and her teacher illustrate what I mean by a continuum of expert learning.

Gracie is a student that puts forth her personal best on any given day. She comes for extra help and makes her journey as a learner visible to her teachers. She typically performs well on most tests, and she has her homework most times. Her daily behaviors exhibit consistent personal high effort. This is why it was evident to her teachers that other factors (unknown to them) were interfering with Gracie expressing her understanding with the academic content that day.

Although Gracie is a student classified with a learning disability, it does not matter. This process of make-up tests is an opportunity Ms. McNally and her co-teacher, Mr. Sands, provide as part of their typical routine for their class assessments as long as students put forth their best effort the first time.

Educators have such an important role in teaching students to be expert learners—teaching each student to be the best version of themselves for these moments in time. Expert learners take charge of their own learning; they are responsible for identifying a purpose, creating and implementing an action plan, and monitoring their learning in ways that keep them on a continuous learning journey by adding new knowledge.

For example, Nick and Jordan enter seventh grade with high expectations for themselves. They have a history of struggling through school. They both start the year off overwhelmed with their new schedules, amount of homework, books, and content to remember. They both attend extra help sessions to practice skills, subjects, and organization of materials and note-taking. As the year moves along, both boys continue to fail many tests. They have a difficult time keeping up with assignments. By March, Jordan has stopped trying. His locker is equivalent to the hallway trash can—and he has lost a few of his textbooks.

Nick has stayed the course. He continues to attend extra help sessions, and he independently applies a note-taking strategy that was taught to him earlier in the year. Nick's grades do not always match his efforts and thoughtful, strategic learning process, but he enjoys school and loves to learn, and he has gained a newfound interest in learning about history and science. His parents are not pleased with his failing grades but admit they see a "new kid." After receiving a failing grade, Nick makes test corrections and identifies a strategy that could help him study and transfer the information the next time. Over time, Nick has demonstrated his true expert learning abilities. He has a clear purpose for learning that motivates him to gain the knowledge and seek the resources he needs. In addition, he identifies with strategies that work for him to achieve his goals.

In any classroom, but particularly in a co-taught classroom, teachers can create expert learners that go way beyond what a grade on a test, assignment, or report card states. According to the UDL Guidelines (CAST, 2018), an expert learner is resourceful and knowledgeable, strategic and goal-oriented, and purposeful and motivated. (See Table 2.1 for the characteristics of expert learners.)

TABLE 2.1. Characteristics of Expert Learners Through the UDL Lens

Learners who are engaged are:	Learners who gain meaning from their perceptions:	Learners who set goals and create an action plan:
• Purposeful and motivated • Eager to learn and motivated by the process of reaching the outcome • Goal-directed—they have a vision for what the end result will be • Open to pushing themselves beyond their comfort zones and challenging themselves to learn more • Resilient and encouraged by the process of learning, viewing setbacks as a natural part of the learning process • Able to regulate their emotions so they can focus on a meaningful learning experience	• Are resourceful and knowledgeable • Tap into their background knowledge base to build upon new knowledge • Seek out and identify resources to help them gain new information • Deepen their understandings by connecting known information with new information	• Identify and apply strategies to organize information • Monitor their performance throughout the learning experience • Decide which strategies work well and which strategies need adjustments to create positive learning experiences

Source: Meyer et al. (2014). Adapted with permission.

Gracie, Jordan, and Nick are all authentic examples of expert learners on very different experiential paths. Clearly, Jordan needed the support to stay connected with himself as a learner. Variables beyond his possible struggles with academic content interfered with his effort to continue trying. So, let's consider tapping into the Ms. McNally and Mr. Sands that reside in all of us; that is, let's consider the ways we meet students where they are, and then support their ongoing personal best efforts along the way. From my experiences, as we do this, students begin to pick up momentum for self-regulating their learning process in ways that portray the expert learner within. Part of embracing expert learning includes understanding the ongoing and evolving balance of fixed and growth mindset in all of us.

CULTIVATING A GROWTH MINDSET

A key to developing learning expertise is to cultivate what Stanford psychologist Carol Dweck (2006) calls the "growth mindset." As we think about learning as a process, we know that the experience will create a variety of emotions. There are times we feel satisfied, proud, and invigorated when our efforts lead to positive outcomes. We get the grade we want, or the product looks like the vision we set out to create. Other times we become frustrated, discouraged, and possibly upset when the results do not meet our hopes or expectations. What constitutes learning? Is it when we have that final product to be proud of to prove, "Hey, I'm good at this!" Or is it the possible failing experience that provides the opportunity to truly learn as we reflect on mistakes and embrace the process of resilient effort that creates the most meaningful learning experiences?

We can all think of a time we succeeded easily at something—just as we can think of a time we struggled. Did you give up during that struggle, or persevere and stay strong to see the learning through? It's our mindset that determines our learning experiences.

Dweck defines *mindsets* as the beliefs that individuals have about their abilities, intelligence, and overall qualities. She distinguishes between growth and fixed mindsets. In a growth mindset, learners believe that as long as they persevere through challenges, their efforts will result in their improving and learning. In a fixed mindset, learners believe that their basic intelligence and abilities are static. They believe people are good at something or they're not, and see effort as a sign of weakness rather than as part of a natural learning experience. A fixed mindset holds that people who succeed are talented. A growth mindset does not deny talent exists but states that success happens through effort and perseverance.

Research supports the idea that students with growth mindsets perform better on challenging tasks than students with fixed mindsets (Blackwell, Trzesniewski, & Dweck, 2007). It is important to note that all learners (all humans, for that matter) do not simply hold either a growth or a fixed mindset. We all experience a blend of both as we go through daily learning experiences.

Mindsets can be learned, practiced, and changed over time, as Dweck's research shows. It is a matter of us becoming more mindful to practice a growth mindset that will enable us to embrace the struggles that go along with meaningful learning experiences. When students are taught that the brain is a muscle that can be developed and in time can become smarter with effort and perseverance, they become intrinsically motivated to put forth their best efforts. Research also shows that the language parents and teachers use greatly influences students' mindsets and performance (Dweck, 2007).

In recent years, Dweck (2015) shared her own ongoing learning about how to implement mindset to guide a meaningful learning process. Here are four clarifications she made:

- Growth mindset is not just about effort. It is about learning and improving. Effort is one piece of an intricate process that includes learners trying new strategies and seeking and applying feedback from others when they experience barriers in learning.

- Focus on the now and the next. Educators should share the specifics of what learners are doing—what they tried—and what they can do next. This emphasizes the process of awareness for current strategies and thinking as learners extend and connect with ways to improve skills, strategies, and outcomes.

- Close personal achievement gaps by being truthful. Let the student know what they are doing well and what they struggle with and provide strategies to help them strengthen their areas in need of improvement.

- Embrace a growth mindset journey. We must remember that individuals are a blend of growth and fixed mindsets. A fixed mindset must be acknowledged as a natural part of the learning process. Once we accept this, we can guide learners (and ourselves) to regulate our emotions away from anxiety and frustration toward acceptance, a sense of calm, and tenacity to apply strategies to meet the challenges in any learning process—resulting in ongoing personal improvement.

MAKING MINDSET A PART OF CO-TEACHING DISCUSSIONS

How does each co-teacher embrace effort and additional practice as part of a natural learning process? Making mindset a part of co-teaching discussions can provide valuable information as co-teachers develop class routines and policies that incorporate the values and beliefs of both teachers. For example, let's look at the following scenario.

Ms. A. and Mr. C. co-teach in a seventh-grade inclusive setting. Mr. C. is mainly concerned with covering the content and giving a test on Friday. Ms. A. knows that the pacing of the material covered along with the reading level present barriers for many students to learn the content. Let's choose an ending to this scenario:

Ending #1
Ms. A. stays quiet, but she provides extra help to students during their lunchtime. These students take the test on Friday and most earn a failing grade. Ms. A. then speaks to Mr. C. to share her thoughts that the class should be given an option to continue studying, make test corrections, and retake the test to show their growth. Mr. C. does not agree and says, "The material was taught, we have to move on—the students should have studied harder."

Ending #2
Ms. A. shares her thinking with Mr. C. She suggests that she incorporate additional scaffolds such as graphic organizers and video, and even have students role-play to demonstrate their understanding of the material. Mr. C. is hesitant because he is concerned about the time. They come to a compromise where scaffolds are added during the instructional time. The students take the test on Friday and most earn a failing grade. Ms. A. suggests that students should make test corrections, continue studying with specific strategies, and retake the test to show their growth. Mr. C. is hesitant, but he remembers how engaged the students were in class. He discusses the situation with Ms. A., who reminds him that the students are becoming stronger at knowing how they learn, and that this additional opportunity not only will boost their confidence and their content knowledge, but also will strengthen their learning habits for future topics and experiences. Mr. C. sighs and trusts Ms. A.'s instincts. All students who received a failing grade are offered the opportunity to do test corrections and retake the test. All students who retake the test pass the test and become more motivated to learn the next topic.

Ending #1 reveals Mr. C.'s fixed mindset as a barrier to guiding meaningful learning. Due to the lack of relationship building between the two co-teachers, Ms. A. tried to guide the students, but without a co-taught team approach, the students were forced into Mr. C.'s fixed-mindset world.

Ending #2 clearly shows how the power of communication between co-teachers may open worlds of opportunities for students as a healthy balance of growth mindset—and willingness to learn is part of the process. It may not be easy to create discussions when each co-teacher has a different perspective, but co-teachers must advocate for all learners in the room. Each teacher must be the voice for all learners and also keep an open mind into different ways of guiding expert learners.

KEY TAKEAWAYS

✔ Being an expert learner *is not* about an end point. It *is* about being open and immersed within a process of learning.

✔ Research supports that students with a growth mindset perform better on challenging tasks than students with a fixed mindset.

✔ All humans experience a blend of growth and fixed mindset. Growth and fixed mindset is not an either/or experience.

✔ Growth mindset is not just about effort—it is about ongoing learning and improving.

✔ You can empower co-teaching relationships by keeping mindsets a part of your discussions.

STUDY GROUP QUESTIONS

1. Describe your understanding of an expert learner. In what ways are you an expert learner? Share one specific example.

2. Think about one past or present student. What specific characteristics, actions, and attitudes serve to define this student as an expert learner?

3. A colleague or parent comes to you and says, "How can you say my (student, child) is an expert learner?! They're struggling in most of their academic classes—that is not my idea of an expert!" How do you respond?

3

Key Idea #3:
Exercising Flexibility as a Means of Addressing Variability

THE POINT OF THIS BOOK is to demonstrate ways co-teachers can structure effective practices and inclusive learning experiences that wholeheartedly embrace the idea of variability. These structures, such as classroom routines and lesson-plan design, provide the opportunity for every learner to feel valued and meaningfully connect with classroom experiences. Co-teachers understand the need to create space for flexibility within decided structures. As co-teachers get to know one another and their students, they will be able to plan with more specificity for the individuals in the room and the context of their particular schools. They will build a sense of community, one centered on the strengths and needs of all learners in the room. You want to do all you can for *each* student in your classroom; that desire will help as you work to understand and apply these powerful ideas. The secret to making this happen is by being flexible in our own thinking. We know our own beliefs and ways of designing instruction but are open to the perspectives of our colleagues, administrators, parents, and, most important, the students in our class.

The classroom is the place to plant the seeds of motivation, where students are engaged and eager to learn through a challenging, memorable, and rewarding process. It's where they hopefully learn to become an expert at the learning process—something they can take with them throughout their lives. Yet for any co-teaching pair, tough questions about implementation abound:

- What do we do for learners who require more supports and scaffolds?

- How do we truly include each learner in our planning and implementation of meaningful learning experiences?

- How do we plan and design instruction that removes barriers, so students are now able to create personal connections and meaning with the content and materials?

Let's review the fundamentals of Universal Design for Learning (UDL) and see how it applies to instructional design and planning. We will not do an exhaustive exposition here—you can find that in *Universal Design for Learning: Theory and Practice* by Meyer et al. (2014).

CREATING SPACE FOR FLEXIBILITY WITH THE UDL PRINCIPLES

In brief, UDL is based on a wide range of research in education practices, cognitive psychology, and neuroscience. David Rose and Anne Meyer (2002), the authors of the UDL framework, identified three brain networks that facilitate a) our intake and processing of information (the recognition network); b) our organizational, decision-making, and communication choices (the strategic network); and c) our engagement, motivation, and ability to persist (affective network).

According to Rose and Meyer, these three networks address the "what, how, and why" of learning:

- Recognition: what
- Strategic: how
- Affective: why

Research shows that there can be a great deal of variability in how each of the networks operate for different learners. These differences in how we are wired can be due to many factors—some biological, some experiential, some emotional. Circumstances can have a big impact: for example, the stress caused by trauma, stereotype threat, bias, or unreasonable expectations can dramatically change the way we perceive information or strategize to perform a task or stay engaged. Context, as noted earlier, is everything.

From these three networks, Rose and Meyer derived the three principles of UDL (Figure 3.1). To address the recognition networks (the "what" of learning), our lessons should provide multiple means of content *representation*. To address the strategic networks (the "how" of learning), we should provide multiple means of *action and expression*, so learners can take on learning tasks and share what they know in the best way possible. And to address the affective networks (the "why" of learning), we should provide multiple means of *engagement*, so learners can get motivated, stay engaged, persist, and self-regulate their learning. Doing all of this will help them become independent, successful learners.

Multiple Means of Engagement
- The "why" of learning
- Affective network
- Options for engaging students in the learning process

Multiple Means of Action and Expression
- The "how" of learning
- Strategic network
- Options for multiple ways learners may express their understanding

Multiple Means of Representation
- The "what" of learning
- Recognition networks
- Options for multiple ways learners may take in and process information

FIGURE 3.1. The three UDL principles and corresponding learning networks

When planned proactively and implemented with flexibility, UDL-based lessons give learners opportunities to enter the learning process through many entry points of understanding. So, for example, if one student has difficulty reading grade-level texts, scaffolds are built into the instruction to support and build comprehension. There is no such thing as "can't" in the UDL classroom. It is a "knock down all barriers" approach that supports all students in achieving their personal best. And along this path, learners focus on their strengths while working to compensate for any apparent areas of weakness. Let's face it: All learners have a blend of both, so why not guide students to use their strengths to compensate or strengthen their areas of weakness? For a student who is reading below grade level, why not use their strength in receptive language and provide audiobooks or online tools to provide text-to-speech supports?

Rather than requiring learners to adapt to an inflexible curriculum, we make a flexible curriculum that can adapt to each learner's needs so that in time they can become independent, engaged, and encouraged.

VARIABILITY THROUGH THE UDL LENS

Take a moment to think about a class full of students. Notice the way the chairs, desks, and tables are set up. Notice the lighting and the time of day. What is the topic and general objective of the lesson? Notice the position of the teacher (maybe it's you!) in the room. What are the students doing? What is the teacher doing? Take a minute to write down or sketch your visualization here:

What is your classroom vision?

_____

_____

_____

Here's my vision:

There are 30 students sitting in rows at individual desks. They are in social studies class learning about [insert topic here]. They are facing the teacher who is at the front of the class clicking away at the SMART Board to reveal a variety of facts through colorful images, videos, and bullet-point notes. The teacher asks a few questions. Students volunteer to answer, and all students are directed to "take notes."

Okay, now that we have our visions, let's look at them in terms of the UDL principles of providing multiple means of engagement, action and expression, and representation.

Mapping my vision of the classroom to the principles, here's what I come up with:

Engagement Learners vary in the way they engage with the information. This teacher has it covered. Or do they? The teacher shares videos, visual images, text notes, and their own voice (auditory). But how are the students really connecting? Clearly some learners in that room have other things on their minds—and sitting at their desk quietly, passively listening and viewing, is not working to gain meaningful attention. More needs to be considered to set a purpose and optimize motivation.

Action and expression Learners vary in the way they express their understanding. The teacher aims to engage the class by tossing a few questions to the crowd. But you guessed it—the same students raise their hands. And the directive and expectation to "take notes" works well for about less than half of this class. Some students write random words on the page to make it look good, while many others do not take notes at all. More needs to be considered to guide each learner to be strategic, goal directed, and, dare I say, organized with note-taking!

Representation Learners vary in the way they process information. This teacher can check off many effective ways to represent the information; they included video, audio, images, and texts all on a colorful and prominent SMART Board presentation. But the multiple ways of representing information are not meant to be a checklist kind of process. More factors affect how we guide each learner to manipulate the information to create personal connections to guide transfer, generalizations, and ultimately make it to the background knowledge storehouse in their long-term memory.

Just think about what this knowledge of learner variability can mean to your classroom—or any classroom. Now take it a step further and think about students in the margins (Rose & Meyer, 2002)—that is, students with disabilities, English language learners, students who are gifted and talented, or anyone who does not fit in the big part of the bell curve. Through a UDL lens, teachers plan for variability, not for some "average" student who does not really exist. Neuroscience has proven that learners are very different. There is no way to depict what an "average" student looks like since we know how different everyone is. Average is something that has been created based on historical views. It creates a situation where teachers plan instruction for the "middle" and hope that the students who are above or below average will be able to stay with the class.

However, many students are disconnected, and way too much instructional time is lost. When teachers plan with a UDL lens and plan proactively for variability, those students in the margins are considered part of the variability, and they are not forced to fit into a lesson that is planned for this mythical middle. Lessons are planned for variability—and all students have the opportunity to connect to the learning process in personally meaningful ways.

PREPARING TO TEACH VARIABLE LEARNERS

Given the great range of abilities and diverse needs in the inclusive, co-taught classroom, UDL comes to the rescue with a framework that translates into a mindset to guide us in creating meaningful learning experiences each day. Implementing the co-teaching models is just one layer of effective co-teaching. The co-teaching models alone just touch the surface of planning effective instruction. UDL can serve as the next layer to designing instruction for the wide range of learner variability found in any inclusive classroom. Instructional decisions within the structure of selected co-teaching models must be accessible, relevant, and meaningful in order for learning to take place. The models help us to organize the structure of learning, and our belief in learner variability along with the principles of UDL provide opportunities for us to address the wide range of learners found in our co-taught classrooms. UDL is all about solutions as we seek to connect each learner with deeper levels of learning.

An important part of the mission for all educators is to effectively navigate the swirling path between planning the curriculum (what they have to teach), implementing their instruction (how they will teach), and guiding their students' minds and hearts to become independent successful learners. Learning in any classroom comes with its own set of excitement and challenges. But additional challenges may easily be found in inclusive classroom settings. For example:

- How are the two teachers in the room going to balance and utilize each other's expertise in meaningful ways?

- How will the needs of a very diverse group of learners be met?

- How will the learners in the room be inspired to become ongoing learners who are self-motivated and independent thinkers?

- How will the two teachers make meaningful learning happen with their students?

The answer to these and other challenging questions can be found within the framework of UDL. When the two teachers adopt a UDL mindset that includes proactively planning, implementing, and assessing learning through a UDL lens, sparks fly—magic happens—and everyone (including the two teachers!) continues to grow and learn in meaningful ways.

The promise that UDL can elevate co-teaching through a view of learner variability blends seamlessly with the practice of providing high-powered instructional decisions in the planning and implementation phases. As mentioned earlier and shown in Figure 3.1, engagement, representation, and action and expression are the three UDL principles that provide the opportunity for us to proactively plan for learner variability. These three principles transform our view of planning and implementing instruction into valuing each learner's unique abilities (and neurodiversity) and viewing instruction through a UDL lens.

When UDL strategies are aligned with the learning networks and co-teaching models, instructional capability is expanded to reach all students, so each one has access to meaningfully connect to the content and the process of learning. In addition, the two teachers in the room will have the opportunity to share their personal expertise and be active participants in the instructional process. Table 3.1 shows how the learning networks, UDL Guidelines, and co-teaching models complement one another.

TABLE 3.1. Mapping Co-teaching Models to UDL and the Brain Networks

BRAIN NETWORK	UDL GUIDELINES	EXAMPLE OF CO-TEACHING MODELS
The recognition network Strategies that support the "what" of learning, so learners may recognize the information being taught	Provide multiple examples Outline and highlight key information Include options for recognition through multimedia and other formats	Station teaching or parallel teaching allows options for each teacher to present information in diverse ways, while keeping the same objective and high standards.
The strategic network Strategies that support the learning process, so learners understand *how* to learn	Provide options for strategic thinking and organizing of information Provide ongoing, immediate, and relevant feedback Provide flexible opportunities to practice skills	Station teaching or parallel teaching allows for both teachers to provide options for strategic thinking and ongoing feedback. The occasional, one-teach, one-assist allows teachers to provide students with immediate, relevant feedback as one teacher focuses on instruction and the other teacher assesses and evaluates students' performance. Teaming may provide the option for one teacher to focus on the content while the other teacher focuses on the process of note-taking. The occasional alternative teaching may focus on one teacher pulling a small group to review a concept while teaching a specific strategy to guide learners' understanding.

TABLE 3.1. Mapping Co-teaching Models to UDL and the Brain Networks *(continued)*

BRAIN NETWORK	UDL GUIDELINES	EXAMPLE OF CO-TEACHING MODELS
The affective network Strategies that support engagement, so learners remain motivated and engaged throughout the learning process	Provide options for levels of thinking and levels of challenge Provide options for choice Offer various options for the context of learning Provide supports to guide learners to self-regulate and monitor their performance	Station teaching may enable teachers to provide choice to students and time to guide self-monitoring and executive functioning skills. Teaming may provide the option for teachers to balance out the teaching of the content while ensuring the salience of high standards by supporting the process of thinking needed to master learning targets.

All three networks and all UDL principles and guidelines are well supported within the natural framework of collaborative teaching and learning within all effective co-taught classrooms.

Let's take a look at what this means for our instructional decisions. When we consider that learners are variable in these three ways, we begin to design instruction that takes down any barriers to learning that may interfere between one or more students. Consider the co-teachers in this English class:

Joanne and Sophia are co-teaching (in any upper elementary or secondary classroom) an English lesson that requires learners to read closely to determine main ideas as well as to make logical inferences. Over the course of the week's lessons, students are asked to cite specific text evidence to support their thinking. Using the UDL principles, these teachers would be sure to do the following.

- Provide multiple ways to engage learners by:
    - Creating a comfortable, risk-free feel to the environment
    - Creating opportunities for students to process individually and then share their thinking with peers
    - Highlighting the goals and learning objectives
    - Incorporating personal strategies to guide learners to push through challenges
- Provide multiple means of representation by:
    - Connecting the lesson to previously taught skills, strategies, and/or content (activate background knowledge)

- Highlighting, preteaching, offering vocabulary supports
- Providing multimedia options such as visual aids, use of digital technology, auditory supplements
- Provide multiple means of action and expression by:
  - Offering options for students to express their thinking—allowing for creative ways to express thinking based on their specific learning goal. For example, when locating text evidence, students may speak, write, or underline/highlight.
  - Offering options for access to resources and tools. For example, some students may experience the process of reading on paper, others on a digital version on the iPad, and others by listening to someone read aloud or to a digital audio version.
  - Exposing students to strategies to guide their personal learning strengths and needs. The strategies should guide them for this lesson but also be strengthening their reading skills in general.

As we gain a deeper understanding of UDL, we must use our initial awareness of the UDL principles to embrace learner variability. We must move our awareness and desire to meet the needs of variable learners into the practice of our instructional decisions.

We can be confident that if UDL strategies are embedded in the learning process, all learners, including students with special needs, will meet with success and gain the ability to become more independent learners. Once UDL scaffolds and the use of co-teaching models have removed as many barriers as possible, the co-teachers' minds and time are more focused on recognizing what additional scaffolds and support are needed by students with more intensive needs. We have now created a learning environment where all learners—including those with more intensive needs—have the opportunity to become expert learners.

FOUR COMPONENTS OF CURRICULUM

A great way to understand UDL is to contrast traditional and UDL approaches to the four components of curriculum: goals, materials, methods, and assessment (Meyer et al., 2014). I've found this to be a helpful tool in my own practice. Let's try it here.

Goals

Traditional instructional goals express what the students will be able to accomplish. For example, students will read the nonfiction article on the water cycle and write a one-paragraph summary of the key points and orally present their summary to the class. When goals are stated this way, some students in the class will not be able to achieve this goal.

A UDL goal leaves the means to achievement open-ended. For example, students will learn key facts about the water cycle and will demonstrate their mastery of this information by selecting one of the expression options. Writing the goal in this way lets students personally connect to the content and provides an opportunity for them to demonstrate what they have learned in a manner that guides meaningful learning. Students will be given options for representation to address possible barriers of decoding, or they may choose to use online sources with a text-to-speech program that allows them to hear the text read aloud. If oral expression presents a barrier for a student due to a disability or anxiety, the student may use other ways to demonstrate mastery, such as creating a digital slide or poster presentation.

It is important to distinguish between instructional goals and Individualized Education Plan (IEP) goals. Instructional goals focus on achieving the necessary grade-level content. IEP goals refer to the individualized goals set for the individual student to guide them to strengthen the skills needed to extend their content knowledge. IEP and instructional goals are easily aligned and should always guide the learner to strengthen individualized skills while learning content knowledge. For example, incorporating cooperative learning activities where all students have the opportunity to share their thinking around content knowledge could address an IEP goal of increasing a particular student's ability to work with peers and collaborate. Another example: Having all students complete a note-taking organizer to help gather particular content could simultaneously meet an IEP goal that addresses a particular student's need to increase organization, note-taking, and/or study skills.

Another important point to remember is that sometimes a goal is written and there is not as much flexibility in providing choice for how students may express their understanding. For instance, if a student presents with difficulties in writing, we must still provide opportunities for them to express themselves through written expression. The goal remains with the aim of a written product. However, UDL (with differentiation, of course!) steps into the picture as we become flexible in the process.

We may, for example, provide the student with time to audio-record their ideas and then listen back to their own words as they write. Another one of many options is to provide graphic organizers and other planning tools to scaffold the writing process, leading toward the ultimate (and sometimes inflexible) goal of a written response.

Notice that by creating a goal through this UDL lens, we stay focused on what we are teaching rather than on one fixed way we want students to learn it. Through this UDL perspective, we create a clear path between the content, the strategies, and affective learning processes.

Instructional Materials

It doesn't take much effort to think about what the traditional curriculum materials look like. Unfortunately, a view that quickly comes to mind is rows of learners facing the front of the room with their textbooks, worksheets, or workbooks on their desks. This image can be shattered as we allow UDL to broaden our opportunities and our integration of materials by using digital versions of printed materials, videos, graphic novels, dry-erase boards, musical instruments, and any other multimedia that provides options for multiple means of accessing, expressing, and assessing understanding through the learning process.

Varied font sizes and background colors can be used to enhance visual presentation. Sections of a text can be reformatted to meet specific students' needs. For example, consider reformatting printed material by chunking sections of reading and providing wider margins and space between paragraphs. That way, students can monitor their comprehension in sections to achieve better organization and comprehension. This option addresses the instructional goal of gaining content knowledge, as well as an IEP goal that specifies a student's ability to self-monitor and increase their comprehension of grade-level texts. Text-to-speech features can be used to support students with decoding and comprehension needs.

As UDL parent-advocate and lecturer Ricki Sabia (2008) notes:

An increased use of digital materials will require a paradigm shift in terms of how technology is used in most schools so that more technology is brought into the classroom. This is the perfect time for such a shift since most districts are developing technology initiatives to prepare students for employment in the 21st century. (pp. 15–16)

Teachers who view the materials through a UDL lens believe that all learners in their classroom use the materials to deepen their personal understandings and to demonstrate their knowledge. Materials must be purposeful and meaningful to each learner in the class throughout the learning process.

Methods

What's the first thing that comes to mind when you imagine the learning process in any classroom? For some, it's lecture-style presentations where the teacher is the "sage on stage." That is because traditionally in classrooms all over the world students sat quietly at desks that were placed in rows as the teachers talked and talked. For the moments when students worked in groups, teachers placed them by ability level. Thankfully, less traditional methods are sweeping through schools all over the world.

Methods are generally defined as the instructional decisions, approaches, procedures, or routines that expert teachers integrate into students' current abilities that aim to accelerate and enhance learning experiences. Some examples are as follows:

- Cooperative learning activities
- Optimizing access to technology
- Providing alternatives to visual information
- Providing alternatives to audio information
- Incorporating movement (get students up and out of their seats!)
- Providing opportunities for students to hear their own thoughts, self-regulate their learning, and then share their thinking out loud. Teachers must appreciate students' perspectives and provide opportunities for learners to value their own voice.

A UDL approach involves multiple means of presenting information to address the various ways students acquire knowledge and to keep the students engaged. For example, the lesson could include a short video clip and other visual representations of the concept. In addition, the class could view information from websites on a large computer screen, and books on the topic (that are appropriate for students at different reading levels) can be offered as resource materials (Sabia, 2008).

Educators who plan their lessons through a UDL lens stay flexible and open to meeting the specific needs of learners in their class. Flexible grouping is applied to help meet a variety of learning outcomes. For example, if the goal is to increase decoding and reading fluency, students can be placed in groups with peers who need to gain similar skills. If the learning target is to increase social interactions, mixed ability levels can be grouped together to allow peers to learn from one another. In addition, a mixed-ability grouping can provide opportunities for each member to express their personal strength. A student who is weak in decoding may be given the role as group illustrator as they listen to their peers share content knowledge. Educators must take a collaborative approach to developing methods in UDL style. The school's librarian or technology experts as well as other teachers are great resources in planning to meet the needs of variable learners.

Assessment

An immediate response to the term *assessment* might be the traditional paper and pencil, multiple choice, open-ended short response, and any end of a unit or chapter source for gaining information about what the learner has grasped. Many problems occur when we use only these summative kinds of assessments to determine whether students have learned. For starters, the content on the test will most likely not align exactly with the instructional process. Additionally, the formatting of the test and the mode of response will not align with the needs of all learners.

A UDL approach to assessment favors formative assessments that provide meaningful data on how students are performing—in real time—within the moments of learning process. Formative assessments provide meaningful, process-oriented feedback to guide all learners to deeply understand themselves as learners. We can collect work samples such as exit tickets, graphic organizers, and writing samples to determine and provide evidence of students' abilities and applications. In addition, techniques are available to us that we can insert in the moments of instruction to gain instantaneous feedback on student engagement and performance. These techniques include ways of getting all students to respond—such as "thumbs up if you agree, thumbs down if you disagree."

Of course, the UDL approach also encourages using multiple means of ensuring that assessments are an accurate and fair measure of what students really know. A quick verbal check for understanding might be more effective than a written quiz, or vice versa. Assessments are also an integral part of sustaining perseverance and resiliency so each learner in the room takes ownership for their learning as they push through the inevitable challenges that any successful learning experience endures.

KEY TAKEAWAYS

✔ Educators address variability when they are flexible in their own thinking. They embrace themselves as expert learners of their content area and pedagogy.

✔ UDL principles provide a reliable structure, grounded in research, to allow educators to proactively design classroom learning.

✔ UDL Guidelines and the three brain networks align seamlessly with the co-teaching models.

✔ Four components of curriculum are considered as we design instruction through a UDL lens: goals, instructional materials, methods, and assessment.

STUDY GROUP QUESTIONS

1. Addressing variability requires educators to be flexible in the ways they think about designing instruction. Think of a recent or upcoming lesson. How were you flexible in your thinking when designing for specific groups of learners? What challenge(s) did you encounter in your own ability to be flexible?

2. How do the UDL principles support your ability to be flexible in your thinking as you design instruction? What is one example?

3. How do you connect the four components of curriculum with the UDL principles and what you know about the co-teaching models so far?

Key Idea #4:
Applying Multiple Structures: A Review of Co-teaching Considerations and Six Models

TO THIS POINT, we've considered the variability of learners, the goal of developing expertise in learning, the ways that UDL can help us achieve that, and the ways that UDL plays out generally across the four components of curriculum. Now, before we consider how this all fits together in the context of co-teaching, let's review what co-teaching is and some common challenges facing co-teachers. Mind you, the definition is changing from decade to decade.

In the past, we defined co-teaching specifically as having one general and one special educator joining together to plan and deliver instruction (Cook & Friend, 1995). In recent years, the definition of co-teaching has expanded beyond the special and general education pairing. Bacharach, Heck, and Dahlberg (2007) define co-teaching as any two teachers working together to plan, organize, deliver, and assess the instructional process within the same shared space. Districts now explore co-teaching arrangements with certified teachers from various backgrounds and disciplines. For example, co-teaching may now include two different content-area specialists, such as an English teacher and a social studies teacher. Moreover, the pairing of general educators with multilingual teachers continues to expand our ideas of what co-teaching is. The history of co-teaching also includes the model of student teachers teaching alongside their cooperating teacher while journeying through the process of becoming certified.

As the notion of co-teaching evolves to include the expertise of additional perspectives and backgrounds, dynamic partnerships in teaching and learning emerge. So, the question becomes: *Where are we now, and where do we want to be in our co-teaching lives?* More important, I wonder: *What kind of experiences do we want our students to have when they are learning in a co-taught classroom environment?* Since writing the first edition, I have personally experienced these changes in co-teaching and have seen it embraced by educators, administrators, parents, and students.

We continue to be on the path of seeking more consistent and accessible learning experiences for all learners in the room—including the two teachers. As we consider making ongoing improvements within co-teaching experiences, it is always good to consider our personal experiences and belief systems.

Too often, inclusion and co-teaching are used synonymously. We hear statements such as "I'm an inclusion teacher"; "My child is in the inclusion class"; "These are inclusion students." This is just plain wrong. There is no such thing as an inclusion class, inclusion students, or an inclusion teacher. Inclusion is not a place or a program. It is not a way to describe students, a teacher, or a class. Inclusion is an idea and a philosophy. It is a belief system that embraces the reality that diverse individuals are included within a positive learning environment. Co-teaching, on the other hand, is a service delivery as a means to provide students with additional scaffolds, supports, and specialized instruction within the general education setting (Friend, 2016). Inclusive settings embrace the variable needs of learners, and students' needs are met within the delivery of a co-teaching model.

THE CO-TEACHING EXPERIENCE

A couple of key components are always visible in the most successful co-taught inclusive settings:

A shared vision Each teacher is connected with their personal philosophy and beliefs about what is right for students. With this solid, personal understanding, each teacher must be open to the perspective of the other teacher. When philosophies are in sync and naturally aligned, life is beautiful, and a smooth road to co-teaching is clearly paved. However, co-teachers who have different beliefs can also share a vision and focus by communicating their personal beliefs and discussing the factors that must be addressed in order to create a clear path. Active listening, communication, and compromise are essential to clearing a path for a successful learning environment. (See the Shared Vision Planning Page in the appendix.)

Active expertise from both teachers General education and special education teachers have shared as well as unique qualities that must be nurtured and present throughout the school year. Figure 4.1 depicts the uniqueness and the overlap of the areas of expertise.

Expertise of Special Education Teacher

- Learning process and strategy
- Differentiated instruction (DI)
- Specially Designed Instruction (SDI)
- Small-group and behavior management
- Data collection and progress monitoring
- Embedding skills to be mastered within the teaching of content

Expertise of General Education Teacher

- Content knowledge
- Classroom management
- Understanding of neurotypical learners
- Pacing of general education curriculum, materials, and grade-level expectations

FIGURE 4.1. Balancing different areas of expertise

As we think about current trends as well as the future of education, it is not too difficult to see that the distinguishing line between general education and special education begins to blur. All teachers need to align the deep learning through a rigorous and exciting curriculum as well as ensure that we are guiding and supporting our students for a successful future.

General education teachers need to have some of the qualities that a special education teacher possesses. For example, general education teachers must become savvy, with a repertoire of strategies that can meet the needs of diverse learners. In addition, they must have the understanding, tools, and ability to apply progress monitoring techniques to guide meaningful learning for all students.

Special education teachers must have the content knowledge to be able to implement high-quality instruction within the framework of district, state, and national initiatives and effective classroom management skills within the co-taught classroom. And so, it is no secret: We need one another. Collaboration, respect, and ongoing communication are necessary to ensure that each teacher is committed to the learning journey in the classroom.

Let's step back in time for a moment. Consider your experience with co-teaching. Let yourself connect with your past for a few moments. Then come back and continue reading.

Here's how my co-teaching experience began. I entered the classroom to meet my co-teacher. She was busy filing some papers and organizing some books on a shelf. As I walked in and introduced myself (all smiles, extended hand), she looked up from her books, tilted her head to allow herself to glance at me from the top of her glasses, and said, "Hi, it's nice to meet you."

She shook my hand in an obligatory fashion—with less than two seconds of eye contact and a loose grip—and then went back to filing and shelving. She responded to comments and questions I posed, and she asked me a few questions as a gesture to get to know me as well, yet I couldn't help but feel like I was in the way. I was invading her space. Her tone, her body language, and her complete indifference was felt and seen. Without speaking, she made it clear she had greater things to do—more important people to speak with—and I knew she wanted to be anywhere but there, with me.

When the air became too thick for either of us to chisel through, I said, "Well, it was very nice to meet you, and I am looking forward to working with you this year." I wasn't lying; I meant every word. But I was a bit deflated. My vision of collaboration and co-teaching were not following the smooth pathway I envisioned. As I was walking out, she called me back into the room.

Here's what she said: "I'm sorry if I do not seem as enthusiastic as you do. This is my third-year co-teaching, and the first two years left me feeling very discouraged. I worked with the same co-teacher the last two years, and it didn't work out. It wasn't her fault or my fault—the system got in the way. She was often pulled for meetings, and we never had any time to plan together. It was so overwhelming to guide struggling learners through grade-level expectations. It's just heartbreaking. Maybe you're right that this will be a good year for us, but I wouldn't count on it if I were you."

My view of co-teaching broadened tremendously in those moments. I interpreted her ability to disclose her thoughts and experiences to me as a positive sign that we would work very well together. After all, my hope for open and ongoing communication had already begun—and it was only the first day!

Stages of Communication

For open and ongoing communication to occur between co-teachers, it will help to recognize three stages in the relational process between any two co-teachers, as suggested by Gately and Gately (2001). In the beginning stage, both co-teachers are guarded and hesitant to collaborate and communicate—the "elephant in the room" kind of feeling that typically results in rigid, less-than-comfortable learning environments. The students feel this tension and, therefore, may not feel that each teacher is a valued educator, individually and as a team. Typically, the teacher who appears to be the lead is seen as the "real" teacher, creating a sense of the other teacher as a "helping" teacher. Next is the compromising stage. This experience provides both teachers with some comfort to share their individual perspectives through emerging communication that allows a sense of give and take to unfold. As long as there is a balance between each teacher compromising—and each teacher feeling valued—then they may progress to the final stage of collaborating. This is the harmonious stage to aim for! The collaborative stage describes each co-teacher valuing the thoughts of their partner. There is an open and ongoing communication process that results in mutual and interactive respect.

With the aim of experiencing the collaborative stage throughout the year, co-teachers must first acknowledge which stage they are really in—beginning, compromising, or collaborative. There is no rush to get to the collaborative stage. Teachers must embrace—in fact, dare I say, celebrate—where you are! Yes, you heard me! Celebrate your awareness to acknowledge exactly how you and your co-teacher are feeling. That is the entry point of your commitment to improving, evolving, and transforming your current and future co-teaching practices. So, let's jump into a reality check—otherwise known as some all-too-familiar co-teaching challenges.

Common Challenges

Co-teaching has been practiced for many decades. Yet today's co-teachers often experience the same problems their predecessors did years ago. Limited or non-existent communication routines, a lack of common planning time, differences in teaching styles and background knowledge, scheduling glitches, difficulties meeting the needs of diverse learners, and lack of administrative supports are just some examples (see Part 3 for solutions with administrators). Many argue that co-teachers must stay together over time to overcome these barriers. But I argue that our students don't have time for that. We must make it work *now*. *This* year. For *this* group of students. It is also unrealistic to think that every co-teacher can be scheduled together each year. We must turn our minds to seeking solutions. What can *we do* now? We must identify surefire ways to make co-teaching—and any co-teaching pairing—work, no matter what. As we begin to do so, let's visit two classrooms.

Co-taught Classroom #1 (Any Grade, Any Subject, Anywhere)

Focus Anchor Standard: Determine central ideas or themes of a text and analyze their development; summarize the key supporting details and ideas.

Twenty-five students sit in rows listening to one of the teachers read aloud from a chapter book. The teacher walks up and down the rows as she dramatically reads and makes eye contact with each student. She uses her voice to guide students to visualize character traits and story elements. She pauses every so often to remind students to close their eyes and visualize. There are no external visuals. There are no additional materials. Just one teacher, rows of desks, and students sitting at their desks encouraged to use their imaginations. The students are visibly attentive as they watch the teacher read with some dramatic displays of expression and voice. A few chuckles can be heard around the room as she reads.

The second co-teacher at the back of the room follows along in his copy of the book—ready to take over the reading as the first teacher nods and smiles his way. Before this second teacher reads, he asks the students a few guided questions to make sure they are following along and understand what's happening in the text so far. These questions are orally presented to the entire class. There are no visuals and no additional materials.

The students are still sitting in their seats. This teacher also walks around the room, so all of the students are once again seemingly attentive. A few students eagerly raise their hands. Some quickly look down at their shoes as the teacher walks past their desk. One or two students are called on, the answers to the comprehension questions are revealed, and the teacher succinctly sums up what has happened in the reading so far. He is ready to continue reading. Students once again follow the teacher's movements and smile as he, too, reads with dramatic expression. At the end of the reading, the first teacher says, "Great class today! Be ready for a quiz on this chapter at the beginning of our next class." The teacher quickly directs the class to transition to the next subject.

Co-taught Classroom #2

The class of 25 students is sitting in groups of five. Students' desks are facing one another. The first teacher is up at the SMART Board reviewing some active reading strategies. She opens a discussion on how to annotate the text to deepen the readers' comprehension. The second co-teacher takes the lead and tells the class they will be practicing this annotation skill during the reading of a short paragraph, as he models his thinking and annotating.

The first co-teacher asks each group to discuss what they noticed about the teacher's think-aloud and how it connected to their own thinking. Students are given a few minutes to discuss. Following a quick debriefing, the first co-teacher introduces the text they are about to read. She offers students a choice. They can read the text while following along with text-to-speech software, they can engage in a shared reading with one of the teachers reading aloud, they can use iPads to read the text electronically (and benefit from dictionary apps), they can partner-read with a peer, or they can go solo and read silently. This may sound like a lot of choices, but these students are used to making decisions for how they will learn best. Their opinions, feelings, moods, and voice are valued each day.

The classroom is set up for the ease of arranging desks and students have the flexibility to choose the process for engaging in the learning experience. As the students move seamlessly around the room, all are ready to begin the reading task within a few minutes. Assigning student groups is not necessary. Thirteen students choose to go solo and complete the reading assignment successfully on their own, while using the iPads occasionally to support their vocabulary knowledge. Five students sit in a group, with one of the co-teachers reading as they follow along. Two students choose to partner-read, whereas five students choose to go to the computer lab, where the librarian has set them up to read along using Google text-to-speech supports. The second co-teacher is monitoring the engagement of all students and implementing supports as needed. He notices that all students are engaged and taking charge of their own learning.

...

There you have it: two classrooms with co-teachers implementing the same lesson in two completely different styles. These two classrooms unveil many challenges experienced in any co-taught classroom. And they also reveal many possible solutions.

What is your first impression? Are both classrooms applying effective instruction? Why do you think the way you do? Are you able to identify the co-teaching models of instruction in each classroom? Regardless of where you are in your understanding of co-teaching, trust your instincts and jot down your initial thoughts here:

First Impressions

Evidence of effective instruction in both classrooms:

_____
_____

Evidence of co-teaching models:

_____
_____

Evidence of UDL components:

_____
_____

We will return to this reflective discussion in Chapter 11, but don't look ahead—that will just ruin all the fun! As you read through the pages of this book, you will gain a deeper perspective into ways to describe what is happening in each classroom. Allow yourself to visualize and to connect to classrooms you know—maybe even your own classroom. And, equally important, nudge yourself to become sparked with ideas for creating inclusive co-taught classrooms that work—no matter what.

Two Possible Barriers for Effective Co-teaching

It is not a secret: Some co-teachers get along beautifully, but far too many do not. The roadblocks to effective co-teaching experiences fall into two categories:

Instruction

- Dealing with differences in content knowledge and teaching styles
- Meeting the needs of diverse learners

Communication

- Identifying ongoing communication methods
- Creating a realistic common planning routine

Co-teachers often do not agree on instructional and classroom management approaches. Each teacher brings a level of knowledge and expertise that may not be valued by the teaching partner, which often results in one teacher dominating the instructional scene. The general education teacher is often viewed as the content-area specialist, which leaves the special education teacher worrying about stepping out of bounds.

With transparent communication in mind, additional challenges must be mentioned. Let the elephants in the room be welcomed and respectfully escorted out of our co-teaching spaces. As co-teaching expands to include a variety of teachers beyond special educators, general educators are charged with applying co-teaching practices with teachers of English language learners, student teachers, and educators with expertise in other content areas. With this broadened awareness of co-teaching, I add two more relatable challenges that special educators have been grappling with for ages:

1. "We do not have time for that!"
   As general educators are invited (often without a choice) to share their classroom and instructional time, it can be difficult to manage time to include strategies shared by their co-teacher. Along these lines, the thought of making time *and* also changing their familiar routine or instructional practice can easily feel daunting. Oftentimes, each co-teacher feels threatened, muted, or separated from the instructional process.

2. "This is the way I do it."
   As a co-teacher enters the general education classroom, it is clear that their philosophy of teaching and learning will be added to an already existing philosophy established by the general education teacher. So now what? Typically, two possibilities unfold. In the ideal setting, the general educator embraces new ideas and new ways of teaching. In a challenging setting, the general educator's mind is set and unwilling to include ideas from a co-teaching partner. Each co-teacher may feel a sense of frustration as their ideas are questioned.

To address these two additional relatable challenges, we need the following:

Perspective Each co-teacher spends time viewing any given situation from the perspective of their teaching and learning partner. It takes practice and a willful stance to step beyond one's personal viewpoint, embrace another, and synthesize to co-create an environment that embraces individual and collective visions and perspectives.

Transparent communication The value of ongoing communication is an understood necessity. Yet, for communication between co-teachers to be of value in transforming teaching and learning experiences, the teaching partners must develop manageable and agreed-upon practices of sharing their thoughts, feelings, and ideas in productive ways. Shared documents on the computer, a notebook, and even sticky notes can serve to document how each co-teacher contributes and then combines their ideas into lessons and situations that require brainstorming, collaboration, and compromise.

SIX CO-TEACHING MODELS

Learning within a co-taught classroom has the potential to ignite the learning for everyone—including the teachers. There is a balance of teacher-directed and student-directed learning that flows within the structure of six specific co-teaching approaches (Friend & Cook, 2007). Within the framework of learning, the student is at the center of it all. Teachers decide which model will best meet the academic, social, and emotional needs of students within the context of a specific lesson. Co-teachers should consider the value of varying small groups and whole-class learning. This flowing movement of the models has great potential to keep students engaged and connected to the learning moments.

One Teaches, One Observes

One teacher manages the instruction, while the other teacher organizes and implements specific assessment tools to gather data on students' performance. This model should be used occasionally as the need arises.

Example

During a seventh-grade social studies class, Nick intermittently shuts down. He puts his head on the desk and often speaks in a low voice: "I just can't do this."

The general education teacher handles this by ignoring him or asking him to sit up. The special education teacher does not want to draw negative attention to the student's behaviors and often just speaks with him one-on-one during and after class to get him back on track.

Benefits

As one teacher instructs the whole class, the other teacher could complete an ABC analysis to identify the **a**ntecedents, **b**ehaviors, and **c**onsequences. In time, the teachers may analyze the data to identify patterns in activities or student behaviors as a means of effectively addressing and redirecting students within the moments of class time. For example, they may notice that Nick shuts down anytime there is going to be group work or a writing task. With this evidence, the teachers will be able to proactively plan and effectively reduce Nick's disengaged and disruptive behaviors and redirect toward successful social and academic learning behaviors. This model should be used occasionally while both teachers remain mindful that they are active participants with expertise that must be valued.

Station Teaching

This model has great potential, as both teachers are sharing their expertise and teaching responsibilities. It also allows both teachers to plan for the learner variability that exists in every classroom. The benefits of station teaching include the ability to:

- Apply flexible grouping depending on the content and activities
- Create groups that focus on reteaching or preteaching
- Plan for groups based on students' skill level or interests
- Facilitate learning for one group, while another group works independently

Example

In this eighth-grade classroom, one teacher facilitates a station to guide the students to gather and organize their notes on the causes of the Civil War. Students are provided with scaffolded support in their researching efforts. At the next station, another teacher facilitates a station to guide the students to use their notes and text-based evidence to write an essay on the causes and effects of the Civil War. At this second station, students apply strategic thinking to add the details needed to write a well-written, informative essay. The third station is an independent station where students work in pairs or independently to revise and edit their writing. Students also have the option to work solo at their desk to complete the task.

Benefits

In this example, the benefits are varied. Students who are able to work independently have the option to work solo to express their skills and knowledge. Students who require support for the writing process are provided with explicit instruction to guide them toward independent researching and writing skills. Students rotate as needed between scaffolded supports and working independently to guide them through meaningful personal learning experiences. Other benefits to station teaching include the following:

- Teachers share content and apply their personal expertise.
- Students receive personalized, customized instruction.
- Students learn strategies and skills to guide them toward independence.
- Teachers can set up rotating stations, allowing all students to experience each station. Or stations may be set up as an option for students to choose their learning process, working toward the same high expectations and learning outcomes.

Parallel Teaching

The teachers divide the class into two groups and facilitate the same lesson with both groups. This model allows learners to receive a more individualized approach, while staying within the comfort of a large group. All learners receive instruction from one of the teachers without rotating groups. Each teacher can address the needs of the learners in manageable ways, and each learner has the opportunity to participate and have access to learning they may connect with personally.

Example

In this third-grade class, the learners are directed to divide up into two groups. One teacher calls out, "Okay, class, let's divide up—north side, go to the front of the room, and south side, meet at the back of the room." As the students move, the teachers wait for students to get settled. Each teacher is prepared to guide students to identify and label the continents on a world map. Although the objective is the same, the process of learning is adjusted to meet the needs of each group. One group uses iPads to give students the option of additional visual and kinesthetic input as they follow the teacher's discussion and map demonstration. Students are engaged by individually connecting to the content on their iPads as the learning unfolds. The other group gains the knowledge of the continents by watching and listening to the teacher's SMART Board demonstration. Students take turns interacting with the SMART Board as the group looks on and discusses the information as a group. By the end of the 45-minute lesson, all students have gained the knowledge necessary to identify and locate the seven continents.

Benefits

This model is a very effective one that can be used frequently to meet the needs of all students. Both teachers are actively part of the instructional process and responsible for all students. Teachers have the ability to individualize instruction in meaningful ways since the group size is manageable. Both teachers have the flexibility to apply their teaching expertise. All students have the opportunity to personally access the learning material as they collaborate with the teacher and their peers while participating in the learning process.

Team Teaching

This model involves two teachers sharing the responsibility of the instruction throughout a lesson. Teaming should be used occasionally to guide whole-class learning, but co-teachers should avoid falling into the trap of both teachers taking on a general educator's role. The special education teacher must be sure to insert specially designed instruction whenever possible. Occasional application of team teaching is best since it can easily result in two teachers generally addressing students as a whole group. Teachers must be careful to make sure that each learner has the opportunity to access and generate meaning from the lesson activities. Each teacher takes on a role to be fully engaged in the delivery of high-quality instruction.

Example

In this seventh-grade science class, one teacher opens the lesson with a brief warm-up activity to get the class ready to learn about the phases of the moon. The warm-up activity requires the group to work in pairs to analyze a graphic that is up on the SMART Board screen. Students are required to simply jot down what they notice. The next teacher takes over and begins to apply the moon phase vocabulary to the students' observations. As one teacher speaks, the other adds comments to repeat or clarify concepts or vocabulary to ensure students' deeper comprehension skills. By the end of the teacher presentation, the students engage in an activity where they demonstrate their awareness of the various phases of the moon by matching a graphic with the specific vocabulary.

Benefits

Teaming is a wonderful option for instruction if your goal is to show parity during the instructional time between the co-teachers. It is also beneficial for one teacher to clarify or repeat any important vocabulary or concepts needed for deeper comprehension. Teachers may model the process of learning as one teacher asks the other questions; this demonstrates to students that successful learners do ask lots of questions as they build their knowledge base. When used occasionally, this is a wonderful alternative that can keep the learning process novel and exciting.

Alternative Teaching

This model is effective for times when some students need specialized attention. One teacher takes responsibility for teaching the large group, while the other teacher facilitates learning for a small group. This small-group instruction may be preteaching, reteaching, remediation, or just additional practice. The large group would engage in a review lesson or individual or group work that is fine for the small group to miss.

Example

Ms. M. guides students to work in pairs to practice identifying text details to support their thinking in response to reading. As students work in pairs, Ms. M. provides additional supports as needed. Mr. G. works with a group of four students at a side table to reteach a strategy to guide students to deepen their independent comprehension skills.

Benefits

This model should be implemented only occasionally and with careful thought. For starters, the same students should not be pulled into a small group all the time. The teachers may rotate who monitors the whole class and who provides direct instruction and additional practice in the small group. When the model is implemented in this manner, students feel comfortable receiving additional support within a comfortable learning environment.

One Teaches, One Assists

One teacher takes the lead for teaching the lesson while the other teacher monitors students' participation and understanding by circulating around the room. Students receive side-by-side additional support as needed.

Example

During this math lesson, one teacher is leading the class through the content. The other teacher walks around the room with a mini dry-erase board to review and reteach the concept as needed for individual students.

Benefits

Students who need additional examples or explanations may receive this support. However, it can also be a distraction as one teacher and one student have a side conversation. In addition, as this additional support is being implemented, the student may fall behind on the whole-class lesson.

MODELS AS A STARTING POINT

The co-teaching models ensure that each teacher's expertise will be valued and implemented. Yet using the models alone does not ensure success. Implementing a variety of co-teaching models means that learners are able to experience learning in a variety of ways rather than just receive it by sitting passively within whole-class lessons. Each model of co-teaching creates opportunities for instruction to meet the needs of all students in the groups. Yet effective instructional strategies must be implemented. Let's look at one scenario.

In a seventh-grade classroom, the co-teachers decide to implement station teaching to guide students to read and take notes on the Columbian Exchange. Here's their plan:

Station 1: One co-teacher reviews one type of note-taking, models it for the group, and guides students to apply it to their own notebooks. The teacher scaffolds struggling learners to copy the model provided as a visual support.

Station 2: One co-teacher facilitates the reading of a section in the textbook to add to the students' background knowledge on the topic. Students who have difficulty reading are told to follow along as the teacher reads aloud. All other students may read silently on their own.

Station 3: Students work independently using laptops and complete a graphic organizer summarizing key points from their notes and reading so far.

These co-teachers are proud of their efforts to create active learning to meet the needs of all learners. It could be true that the smaller groups can serve to create more engaged learners—but have they created a more effective learning experience? Let's look at the first station, for instance. Students are guided to take efficient notes, but not only are they told *how* to take the notes, they are also encouraged to just copy from the teacher's model if they are having difficulty. How does just copying help learners be strategic, self-directed learners? The answer: It doesn't.

One very frequent question I receive is: "With so many options for co-teaching models, how do we know which one to use?" Another very common question I receive is: "What happens if we mess up and realize we have selected the wrong model in the middle of a lesson?!" Great questions!

Which Co-teaching Model Should We Select?

When considering the traditional six co-teaching models, the basic rule of thumb is simple. Ask yourself: Is our lesson better delivered to the whole class or small groups? What are the differences? Table 4.1 offers a summary of some things to think about when considering which model to choose.

TABLE 4.1. Considerations for Selecting a Co-teaching Model

WHOLE-GROUP LESSONS	SMALL-GROUP LESSONS
Strengthen class community	May increase students' attention to tasks
Encourage co-teachers to model communication and teamwork	Strengthen a sense of community within small-group connections
Provide opportunity for flexibility as co-teachers share their thoughts and expertise throughout the lesson	Increase students' individual skill set with increased teacher–student and student–student connections
Provide an opportunity for students to actively participate in a whole-group setting and expand their perspectives as they share their thinking and listen to others	Provide opportunities for all learners to actively participate within the lesson and expand their perspective by listening to others in a small-group setting

TABLE 4.1. Considerations for Selecting a Co-teaching Model *(continued)*

WHOLE-GROUP LESSONS	SMALL-GROUP LESSONS
Allow co-teachers to work in tandem and embed their personal style and expertise as appropriate	Allow co-teachers to work in partnership with a strong opportunity to exhibit personal expertise as they facilitate the lesson
May allow one teacher to focus only on students' performance to allow for anecdotal notes as formative assessment	Often increase teachers' view of how students are perceiving the content as well as performing to express what they know
Aligns with: • Team Teaching • One Teaches, One Observes • One Teaches, One Assists	Aligns with: • Station Teaching • Parallel Teaching • Alternative Teaching

That's it! It narrows the choice of six models down to a choice of three (Stein, 2017), as shown in Figure 4.2. Simply glorious, right?!

Whole-Class Choices

- Team Teaching
- One Teaches, One Observes
- One Teaches, One Assists

Small-Group Choices

- Station Teaching
- Parallel Teaching
- Alternative Teaching

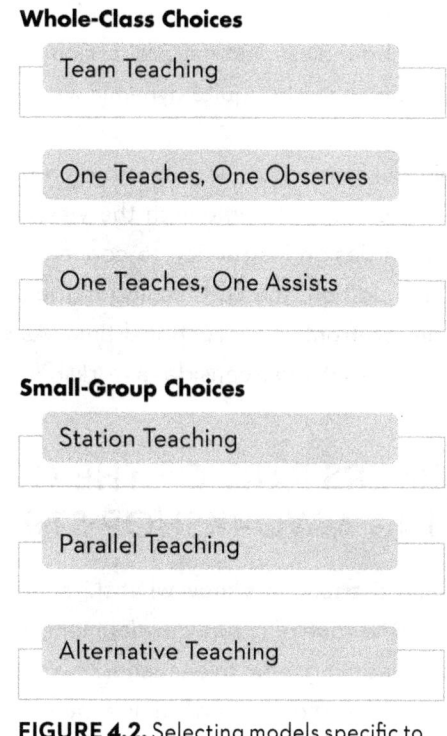

FIGURE 4.2. Selecting models specific to whole-class and small-group lessons.

What if a Model Is Not Working?

As for the question of what to do if (or, quite frankly, when), mid-lesson, co-teachers are thinking, *Oh, no! This is not going the way we planned—this model is not working!* Fear not! This is a natural part of an exemplary co-teaching process as long as the co-teachers stay keenly aware and do one thing: Change it up! Right there ... in the moment.

Be flexible and open to meeting the students and your co-teaching partner where they are in the present moment. This is also an example of a time when the co-teachers' transparent communication must be on solid ground. Right there in the moment—in front of the students—quickly plan for the changes needed.

Think out loud (fishbowl-style), where the students are witnessing real-world collaborations. This way, the co-teachers not only are modeling authentic, necessary, and productive communication and collaboration, but are also improving the process of the lesson together—with their students. In fact, if it feels appropriate, co-teachers could provide the opportunity for their students to be a part of the decision-making process for changing up the structure of the learning in the moment. I am talking about co-teaching heaven here!

The possibilities are boundless and magical for co-teachers to co-create a sense of community in unplanned but quite dynamic ways with all learners in the room.

To provide meaningful instruction, we need to do more. The models simply organize a structure for us to be flexible with the way we group our learners for specific lessons as we design instruction to connect each student with the learning experience. In addition, the co-teaching models allow each teacher's expertise to rise to the forefront of instructional time. As we consider creating space for learners' expertise, let's also consider a workshop model of co-teaching.

MAKING LEARNERS PART OF THE CO-TEACHING TEAM: APPLYING A WORKSHOP STRUCTURE

We understand that effective teachers know what skills their students are able to perform independently (*the zone of actual development, or ZAD*). Knowing each student's entry point for learning, effective teachers plan to guide their students beyond their ZAD and nudge them toward their *zone of proximal development* (*ZPD*; Vygotsky, 1978). In addition to the co-teaching models discussed so far, the workshop structure deserves careful consideration.

A workshop model embraces the powerful "I Do, We Do, You Do" scaffolded structure developed by Lev Vygotsky (1978). Consider the following general lesson outline using a workshop structure (for any subject or grade level):

I Do: Teacher(s) explicitly model a strategy or share knowledge that the students need to know. (10 minutes)

We Do: Teacher(s) invite students to begin to process and apply this knowledge or strategy application. Students begin to make the information their own, and the teacher(s) are guiding the process. (10 minutes)

You Do: Students apply the knowledge and/or strategy on their own, in pairs, or in small groups. (20 minutes)

This workshop structure has boundless possibilities for co-teachers. The first "I Do" section may be structured using one of the six co-teaching models discussed earlier. For example, co-teachers may decide to parallel-teach the first 10 minutes, or they may decide to team-teach as they address the whole class. The most important part of this workshop structure is that the students are given the opportunity to take charge of their learning to the greatest extent possible. During the "You Do" stage, teachers may meet with individual students or in small groups or utilize this time as valuable formative assessment to monitor students' performance.

Note that the time for the students to apply "You Do" should take up most of the instructional time. The principles of UDL connect seamlessly with this workshop model. Learners are engaged and active: They apply strategic thinking as they learn to monitor their understanding and progress. Learning is not about completing tasks to simply comply with teacher directions. It becomes about students' making sense of the content and materials and processing the information at their own pace and level of understanding. The workshop structure provides opportunities for students to connect to learning that goes beyond simply connecting to tasks to complete. Since most of the instructional time allows for high levels of student voice and application, the learning becomes an authentic process.

Questions to consider when applying a workshop model

1. Think about how the workshop structure can elevate the learning in your classroom. How could you specifically apply this structure with your students? What would the 40-minute block of time look like?

2. Why is it important to provide most of the instructional time to the "You Do" phase within the workshop model? How could you and your co-teacher support each other during this instructional time?

3. How does specially designed instruction (SDI) fit with UDL-informed co-teaching?

As the ideas in this book unfold, you will see that it is within your power to improve whatever model you choose by applying the research-based principles of Universal Design for Learning. UDL will allow you to create relevant, engaging, and active learning experiences for all learners in the room. In subsequent chapters, I will show you how to elevate co-teaching by embedding scaffolds and strategies according to UDL principles, and by providing further explicit instruction and scaffolds through SDI to address individual student needs according to their IEPs.

Our goal is to help students see that learning is not a chore but an opportunity for them to experience the joy of personal growth as they push through challenges and expand their comfort zones—something they will be able to do because their teachers have designed these instructional experiences with appropriate scaffolds, and with relevant content and materials.

KEY TAKEAWAYS

✔ Co-teaching may be defined as a dynamic partnership in teaching and learning.

✔ Inclusion and co-teaching are not the same thing. Inclusion is an idea and philosophy. Co-teaching is a service delivery model to support designing specialized instruction in a general education setting.

✔ Co-teaching involves creating a shared vision and ensuring the active participation and expertise of both teachers.

✔ According to Gately and Gately (2001), there are three stages of communication between co-teachers: beginning, compromising, and collaborative.

✔ Common co-teaching challenges include inefficient communication, lack of planning time, differences in teaching styles, and lack of administrative supports (see Part 3 for solutions with administrators).

✔ There are six basic co-teaching models that support whole-class and small-group instruction. In addition, a workshop model may be applied to elevate the expertise of all learners in the room.

✔ The co-teaching models are a structure for organizing groups of students to maximize learning. The models alone do not serve as an instructional strategy. Co-teachers must design all instruction within each lesson and each selected co-teaching model around the students' needs.

✔ Co-teachers may consider the workshop structure that creates time for students to apply and transfer the knowledge and concepts they are learning in class. Any class instruction may be elevated with strategies that connect to UDL with keeping the learner at the center of meaningful learning experiences.

STUDY GROUP QUESTIONS

1. Describe what a dynamic co-teaching partnership looks like and feels like.

2. Why is it so critical for co-teachers to create a shared vision? Do you think students in the class can tell if a shared vision between co-teachers exists? Explain.

3. How do you connect with the idea of the three communication stages? What specific advice would you give to a co-teaching pair who wishes to reach the collaborative stage?

4. How might the UDL principles and guidelines be used as a source for finding solutions to common co-teaching challenges? Share one example.

5. Explain the importance of varying the co-teaching models. How does considering whole-class and small-group lessons guide your implementation of the models?

6. What is one example of when you would apply a workshop model to elevate co-teaching and learning in your classroom?

PART 2

In the Classroom: Partnering With Your Co-teacher and Students

5

Getting to Know Our Students

THE BEGINNING of every school year is an exciting time when teachers plan activities to get to know their students. Interviews, checklists, and class activities are often implemented as everyone works to become a learning community that will set the tone for the year. Sometimes these interviews and inventories are completed and then filed away as the focus centers on the need to teach the content.

As we take time in the beginning of the year to get to know our students, we must remember to continue developing our knowledge of our students even when the pacing of the curriculum sweeps us into a whirlwind of content. In the co-taught classroom, there's an additional need to understand our students. Of course, learner variability exists in any classroom, anywhere. But students in co-taught, inclusive settings typically exhibit such a broad range of abilities that a higher level of planning and implementation is needed to ensure that we are meeting the needs of each student.

CLASS LEARNING PROFILE

One effective tool for guiding a yearlong awareness and application of the knowledge of students' abilities and needs is the Class Learning Profile (Table 5.1, adapted from Rose & Meyer, 2002). This is a powerful way to align the UDL principles into instruction in natural and meaningful ways as we look to educate the whole child. We teach individuals, not subjects. The class profile is an ideal tool for guiding our relationship with students throughout the year. The first column indicates the connection between learning and the three brain networks. The other columns outline the strengths, needs, and preferences of individual students. This is a perfect co-teacher communication tool as well as a source for teachers to refer to as they proactively plan and implement lessons. See the appendix for a blank template of the Class Learning Profile for your personal applications.

TABLE 5.1. Class Learning Profile

NETWORK	STUDENTS' STRENGTHS	STUDENTS' NEEDS	GENERAL STUDENTS' INTERESTS
Affective The ability to push through and understand the purpose for learning along with ability to effectively integrate the emotions involved in learning	*William*: Focused *Matthew*: Enjoys working independently *Rachel*: Works well with peers *Ted*: Asks meaningful questions *Anthony*: Energetic	*William*: To increase coping skills to lessen anxiety *Matthew*: To increase collaboration skills *Rachel*: To increase independent study skills *Ted*: To increase confidence *Anthony*: To increase resiliency to stay with a task when challenging	*William*: Cars *Matthew*: Drawing, dogs *Rachel*: Animals, iPad, video games *Ted*: Music, video games, baseball *Anthony*: Sports, computer graphics
Recognition The ability to perceive presented information	*William*: Aware of his surroundings *Matthew*: Strong background knowledge base *Rachel*: Interprets visual charts, maps, graphs *Ted*: Curious *Anthony*: Attentive when information appears in color	*William*: To increase working memory *Matthew*: To develop word decoding and fluency *Rachel*: To increase word recognition *Ted*: To increase independent inferencing skills when reading *Anthony*: To increase word recognition, fluency, comprehension	

TABLE 5.1. Class Learning Profile *(continued)*

NETWORK	STUDENTS' STRENGTHS	STUDENTS' NEEDS	GENERAL STUDENTS' INTERESTS
Strategic The ability to plan and follow through with an organized process of learning	*William*: Strong listening comprehension *Matthew*: Organized *Rachel*: Flexible and positive outlook *Ted*: Identifies keywords and has strong summarizing skills *Anthony*: Enjoys drawing, sketching, creating mind maps	*William*: To increase reading comprehension (fluency and vocabulary) and written expression (gathering information, organizing ideas, writing sentences, proofreading) *Matthew*: To determine importance when locating keywords, information *Rachel*: To develop self-monitoring skills *Ted*: To increase ability to transition from one idea/topic/activity to the next *Anthony*: To increase independence when paraphrasing and identifying important information	

Adapted with permission from Meyer and Rose, 2002

Through a UDL lens, we acquire this knowledge that every learner has the ability to become an expert learner. That is, each learner has the ability to achieve to their personal absolute best. It is the decisions we educators make that provide the context for learning for all students to experience the process of becoming the best version of themselves as learners. How do we do that? Let's return to the UDL Guidelines (see Figure 5.1). The bottom row outlines the ultimate goal for learners to achieve expert learner status. Ideally, expert learners are learners who are engaged and intrinsically motivated and able to self-regulate. They are resourceful, knowledgeable, and able to comprehend new understandings. Finally, expert learners are strategic, goal-directed, and able to put successful executive functions firmly in place to plan, organize, and follow through with learning tasks to completion (CAST, 2018).

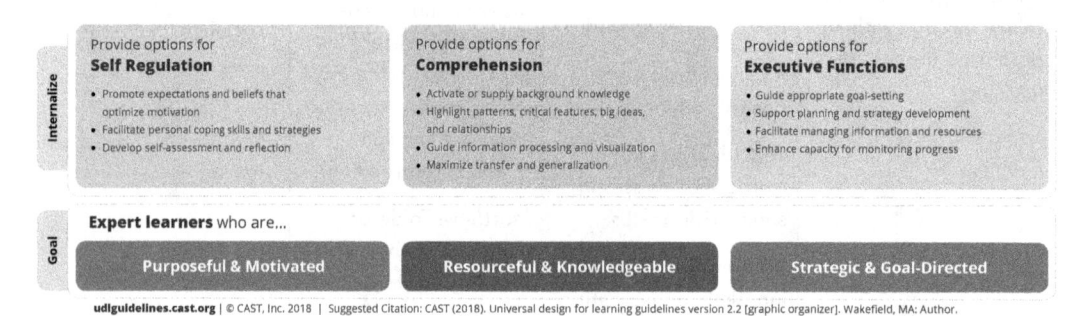

Internalize	Provide options for **Self Regulation** • Promote expectations and beliefs that optimize motivation • Facilitate personal coping skills and strategies • Develop self-assessment and reflection	Provide options for **Comprehension** • Activate or supply background knowledge • Highlight patterns, critical features, big ideas, and relationships • Guide information processing and visualization • Maximize transfer and generalization	Provide options for **Executive Functions** • Guide appropriate goal-setting • Support planning and strategy development • Facilitate managing information and resources • Enhance capacity for monitoring progress
Goal	**Expert learners** who are...		
	Purposeful & Motivated	Resourceful & Knowledgeable	Strategic & Goal-Directed

udlguidelines.cast.org | © CAST, Inc. 2018 | Suggested Citation: CAST (2018). Universal design for learning guidelines version 2.2 [graphic organizer]. Wakefield, MA: Author.

FIGURE 5.1. The UDL Guidelines: The keys to expert learning. © 2018, CAST. Used with permission.

The middle and top rows of the guidelines serve as checkpoints for us to create a positive journey toward each learner's right to become an expert learner. These two rows are checkpoints we can use to make sure we provide opportunities and scaffolds to guide each learner on their personal learning journey (see Figure 5.2).

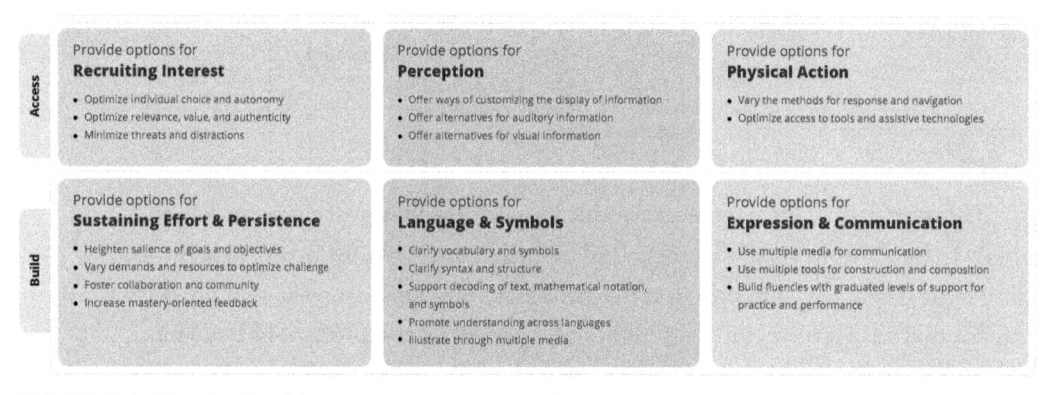

Access	Provide options for **Recruiting Interest** • Optimize individual choice and autonomy • Optimize relevance, value, and authenticity • Minimize threats and distractions	Provide options for **Perception** • Offer ways of customizing the display of information • Offer alternatives for auditory information • Offer alternatives for visual information	Provide options for **Physical Action** • Vary the methods for response and navigation • Optimize access to tools and assistive technologies
Build	Provide options for **Sustaining Effort & Persistence** • Heighten salience of goals and objectives • Vary demands and resources to optimize challenge • Foster collaboration and community • Increase mastery-oriented feedback	Provide options for **Language & Symbols** • Clarify vocabulary and symbols • Clarify syntax and structure • Support decoding of text, mathematical notation, and symbols • Promote understanding across languages • Illustrate through multiple media	Provide options for **Expression & Communication** • Use multiple media for communication • Use multiple tools for construction and composition • Build fluencies with graduated levels of support for practice and performance

FIGURE 5.2. The UDL Guidelines: More keys to expert learning. © 2018, CAST. Used with permission.

STRENGTHS-BASED INVENTORY

In contrast with the concept of innate learning styles (see the sidebar "Why I Don't Talk About Learning Styles"), Thomas Armstrong (2012) draws on findings from neuroscience to emphasize the idea that skills and strengths develop and improve with practice. The brain physically changes as learning happens, and as it does, so does the capacity to learn in all sorts of ways. The findings from the science of neuroplasticity, or changeability, open wonderful possibilities for us as teachers. We can view student variability as an opportunity to help students grow rather than as a barrier we have to surmount. The implications for students in special education are tremendous. We can stop looking at students within the limited box that a classification label too often creates. We can acknowledge that each student has the capacity to grow and evolve into deeper learning as a flexible thinker who creates deeper learning experiences.

One tool to help guide us to get to know our students in an ongoing, meaningful way is the strengths-based approach (Armstrong, 2012). The strengths-based approach originated in the field of social work, where an emphasis on self-determination and the belief that every person has strengths to draw on is applied to the challenges facing particular clients. Armstrong adapts this approach to education. He recommends that in addition to gathering information from parents, previous teachers, cumulative files, and student inventories, we produce a strengths-based inventory for each student.

Inspired by Armstrong's 165-item strengths inventory, I created a quick check-in tool to use with students. This tool not only guides relationship-building between teachers and students but also raises students' self-awareness as learners. The check-in includes the following questions:

1. What is one personal strength that you feel proud of?

2. Describe one way you are effective in communicating with others (for example, speaking, listening, writing, telling stories, or telling jokes).

3. What are your social strengths (for example, demonstrating leadership abilities, being helpful to others, socializing, or showing empathy for others)?

4. What are your emotional strengths (for example, keeping a positive attitude most of the time, being able to push through struggles, accepting guidance from others, or caring for other people)?

5. Name one intellectual strength that you notice (for example, musical; artistic; creative; interested in math, science, nature, reading, or writing).

6. Name one physical strength that you notice (for example, exercise, bike riding, skateboarding, or sports).

7. Tell us more! What other strengths do you have? What hobbies do you have?

(See the appendix for a blank template titled Strengths-based Check-in Reflection. You can use this for your applications.)

This open-ended check-in can be used as a teacher–student interview, or teachers may ask students to complete them independently. I like to give this quick check-in once in September, and then ask students to complete the check-in again in March or April. I recommend having students compare their two check-in reflections and see how they have evolved in their view about themselves over time. It can also serve as a powerful resource to guide students to create summer learning goals, or goals they would like to create for the upcoming school year. Respecting the presence of and providing opportunities for the unique minds (the neurodiverse thinkers) that you have the privilege of working with each day is the foundation of UDL—and it is with this perspective that the value of learner variability is created, and meaningful learning breathes through the classroom each day.

Again, the strengths-based inventory is a tool that can open possibilities to more flexible education, not lock students into ideas of what they can or cannot accomplish. It serves as a quick survey to help learners build self-awareness. Learning will really take off in the co-taught classroom when both teachers recognize that every student has strengths, every student can learn, and every student can learn to learn—that is, to become an expert learner.

KEEPING VARIABILITY IN MIND THROUGHOUT THE YEAR

Let's be real—the life of a teacher gets busy. Multiply that by two, and you have a very busy co-teaching year. The demands may cloud your focus on keeping the natural variability (and notion of expert learning!) in mind throughout the year. Are you ready to hear the secret (which is really no secret) of attending to variability and sustaining the mindset needed to embrace the expert learners in your room (including you and your co-teacher!) throughout the days, weeks, and entire school year? The UDL action steps shown in Figure 5.3 provide the structure and flexibility you need.

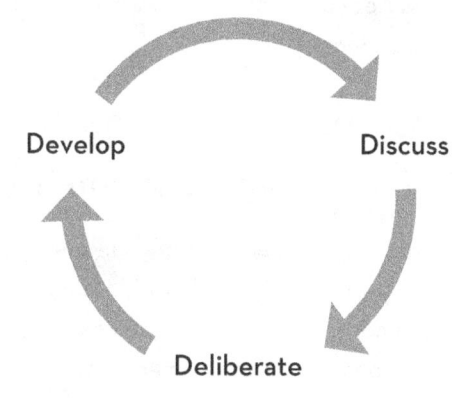

Develop → Discuss → Deliberate → (cycle)

FIGURE 5.3. UDL action steps

1. **Develop** a manageable planning process that works for you and your co-teacher. Make sure it is a plan that provides incremental successes along the way; this will be embedded motivation to keep the plan moving. The planning process should be simplified in a way that maintains the flexibility to sustain consistent, transparent communication.

2. **Discuss** the plan. Once you and your co-teacher agree to it, this will become the framework for your iterative planning process. This process will provide a structure with the necessary flexibility embedded to ensure that no matter what happens in the busy daily in and out of the school days and weeks, you will manage to fine-tune and maintain your co-teacher connection.

3. **Deliberate** and hold each other accountable. Give each other feedback and adjust along the way based on that feedback. Also, remember to include your students in the process of your planning—get feedback from them! After all, as we embrace UDL, we acknowledge that we are all learners and therefore will learn so much from our students as well.

As co-teachers embrace the concept of variability, an awareness of students' varying abilities becomes clearer. The UDL principles illuminate the ways that individuals and groups of learners vary in how they connect, perceive, and express themselves within the wide array of content and lesson activities. Considering the context of learning becomes an organic part of designing lessons through a UDL lens. As the context of learning is recognized, educators understand that although learners have learning preferences (visual, auditory, kinesthetic), no learner is ever just one type of learner. Context matters. Our learning preferences hold true along a variety of sensory pathways depending on specific learning environments and experiences.

▶ Why I Don't Talk About Learning Styles

Once we embrace the idea that all learners can become expert learners, we begin to realize that all meaningful learning is contextual. We learn to design lessons that encourage students to be flexible thinkers. We do not want to make assumptions (and create unnecessary and unintentional barriers!) by labeling our students as certain types of learners or by assuming that they have certain learning styles that determine whether they can become experts. Many teachers consider a student's "learning style" as they plan a lesson. Yet, as we have learned from the work of Daniel Willingham (2021), we can wonder whether learning styles exist at all. We know students have learning strengths, but to say that any particular learner is one fixed type of learner or another is a form of classifying students and interferes with a clear pathway to learning.

From a UDL perspective, meaningful learning happens within a context. So, if we embrace a traditional learning style approach and say that Tim is an auditory learner, his teachers—but more importantly, Tim himself—will consider this to be true. So, in all his classes, his teachers are sure to provide additional auditory input. Yet, by considering the learning style over the context of learning, well-intentioned teachers often create inadvertent learning barriers. Quite frankly, there are times when Tim benefits from additional visual or kinesthetic modes, despite an understood auditory strength.

For example, let's consider Tim in his sixth-grade English class. The text the students are reading is supported by an audio CD to reinforce the comprehension for a few learners in the class. That works out well for Tim. That same day, Tim goes to social studies class, and the teacher makes certain to provide additional auditory cues through her lecture and student discussions to reinforce students' understanding of the geography of the 13 colonies. Tim seems to understand the content. The next day, Tim is able to transfer his comprehension in English class, but he does not retain the information in social studies. The social studies teacher is heard telling the English teacher, "I don't get it. I provided additional auditory to support his understanding of the geography of the 13 colonies, and he is still struggling. Maybe he didn't study enough. He will have to come for extra help at lunch."

From a UDL perspective, when the context of learning is considered, we realize that although learning style strengths are evident, it is the context of learning that drives true learning. Providing multiple means of representation gives students like Tim the opportunity to utilize the modality they need in the moments of that lesson. We need to consider what we are asking students to know and be able to do and provide learning pathways accordingly. In the case of the geography lesson, all Tim needed was additional visual cues—an additional map to view and a blank one to complete—to strengthen his understanding and transfer of the content. If additional visual and perhaps kinesthetic input was provided in the moments of that lesson, Tim would not have needed to miss his lunch period to review content that was made unintentionally inaccessible during the moments of class time. It's all about embracing variability in the context of learning.

✔ Co-teaching Check-In Activity

Stop, Jot, and Share: What Kind of Learner Are You?

Learning how to learn means many things. It means learning how to prioritize one's attention, time, responsibilities, and preferences. It also means learning what strengths and weaknesses we have and the methods that support our ongoing learning and improvement.

Think about what kind of learner you are. What are your perceived strengths and areas in need of improvement? What kind of learning do you enjoy most? What content-area subjects get you most excited about learning?

Now share your thoughts with your co-teacher. Either have a discussion, or share your written responses and read each other's perspective—or both!

KEY TAKEAWAYS

✔ Variability exists everywhere learners gather. Yet, students in a co-taught, inclusive setting typically exhibit a broader range of abilities and areas in need of skill development.

✔ The Class Learning Profile is one tool that serves to get to know your students at the beginning of the school year and should be updated as necessary along the way. It also serves as lesson designing tool all year round.

✔ The strengths-based inventory is another tool to guide getting to know our students. It taps into learners' strengths—from the students' perspectives—to guide teachers to use strengths as a way to lift areas in need of improvement.

✔ The UDL action steps—Develop, Discuss, Deliberate—provide ongoing opportunities for co-teachers to structure their co-planning focus while keeping variability in mind through the school year.

✔ Shifting our thinking away from the notion of learning styles toward variability and context promotes personal, accessible, and meaningful learning experiences for individuals and groups of learners.

STUDY GROUP QUESTIONS

1. Thinking about the notion of variability, what is the range of abilities that are present in your classroom?

2. Discuss at least three ways you would benefit from completing a Class Learning Profile. How will that specifically benefit you and your students throughout the year?

3. How does the strengths-based inventory potentially ramp up your co-planning, co-teaching, and co-assessing process throughout the year? Explain how students' perspective increases teachers' awareness of designing and implementing thoughtful lesson designs.

4. How might the Develop, Discuss, Deliberate process empower you and your co-teacher? Share a specific scenario for applying this process.

5. Explain how learning preferences, variability, and context are key in moving beyond the rigid notion of learning styles. Why is this evolution of thought so important? Are you ready to remove learning style thinking? Your students will thank you!

6

Planning Powerful Instruction

IT IS IMPORTANT for co-teachers to remember that the instructional decisions they make greatly impact students' belief in themselves as learners. The flexibility and goal-oriented nature of UDL empowers learners, and co-teachers have the opportunity to create meaningful learning experiences. Effective co-teaching experience begins with teachers who share a vision for the purpose and goals of learning while combining their individual expertise. It moves on to unfold into a meaningful process of active learners all striving to reach specific learning goals through a pathway that makes sense for them. Finally, throughout the entire learning process, both teachers are monitoring (and guiding students to self-monitor) their performance. It is through these keen observations and monitoring that learning becomes intentional and motivational. These observations and evidence of students' performance guides all instructional decisions in real time.

When co-teachers plan and combine their expertise, they are following their general lesson plan outline. They consider the goals for the lesson and the instructional decisions about what strategies they will use to keep the process of the lesson moving. In addition to the process of instruction, they consider the way(s) they will incorporate formative assessment to monitor the students' abilities and performance. When each teacher adds their ideas for how to meet the needs of each learner, the chance for student achievement is greater. When there is a balance of decision-making and responsibilities between co-teachers, they can provide multiple means of effective co-teaching to optimize the process through a UDL lens.

Enter specially designed instruction (SDI).

BLENDING SPECIALLY DESIGNED INSTRUCTION AND UDL PLANNING

SDI is what special education teachers are trained to do—to create specialized instruction to meet the needs of particular learners. SDI is the thoughtful process of designing instruction by adapting the content, methodology, or delivery of instruction to accommodate a learner's disability. These adaptations ensure access to the general education curriculum so that learners may participate in the learning process as they work toward goals and expectations outlined in their Individualized Education Plans (IEPs) as well as in district expectations and learning standards.

SDI is a planned, organized, and meaningful process that intentionally and systematically addresses the student's needs as expressed in the student's IEP. Weiss et al. (2020) found that special education teachers in co-teaching partnerships believed they were implementing special education through their co-teaching model; however, they could not identify evidence of SDI in their daily instruction. This is a good place to remind you that co-teaching is a structure—it is a delivery model within a classroom. But what happens within the classroom? What does the instruction look like? Friend (2015) calls for an increased awareness in what co-teaching is and how it is experienced: "Instead of just providing on-the-spot prompting and coaching simply to get students with disabilities through the academic content at hand, the most effective co-teachers now also provide the same kind of explicitly designed and carefully documented instruction that has always characterized special education" (p. 18). Figure 6.1 illustrates how SDI may be embedded within daily

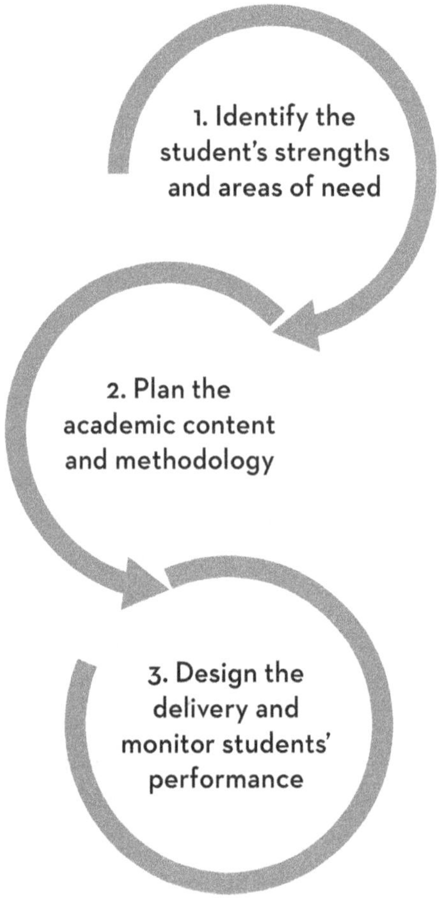

FIGURE 6.1. The flow of SDI

1. Identify the student's strengths and areas of need
2. Plan the academic content and methodology
3. Design the delivery and monitor students' performance

instruction in a manner that goes beyond simply prompting and fitting a student into the lesson. It is about designing curriculum that aligns with the students' abilities and areas in need of improvement.

Effective instruction always begins with knowing our students (use the Class Learning Profile from Chapter 5 to organize your thinking). We know their strengths and needs and use those to strengthen the areas in need of improvement. Once we know our students, that is the entry point to introduce the content (general education curriculum). In addition, the co-teachers must decide how they are going to teach the content. What is the structure? How will you organize the lesson? Enter the co-teaching models from Chapter 4. Finally, the co-teachers must carefully select instructional strategies that scaffold and guide the students to be resourceful, confident learners. SDI is explicit, systematic instruction that meets the students where they are and guides them to strengthen their skills and knowledge base. Specially designed instructional decisions are based on specific needs outlined on a student's IEP, and through a UDL lens we know that what is necessary for one student is often good for many learners. Table 6.1 illustrates further details and examples of SDI.

TABLE 6.1. Examples of SDI

CONTENT	METHODOLOGY	DELIVERY OF INSTRUCTION AND PROGRESS MONITORING
General education curriculum and state standards	The structure of instruction	How are the students' needs met (for example, more explicit, more systematic, and embedding formative assessments to monitor students' performance)?
Academic content—for example, textbooks; websites; reading passages; math workbooks; literacy programs; and science, social studies, and all content-area materials	Examples include: • Co-teaching models • Chunking the learning by segmenting into smaller sections to allow processing time • Cooperative learning activities • Project-based learning	Examples include: • Preteaching and reteaching skills or content • Teacher modeling • Explicit step-by-step instruction • Use of software to guide learning process • Graphic organizer to help plan thinking for writing • Formative assessments (see Chapter 3) to get a sense of students' progress

This specialized focus must link with the general education curriculum and learning targets. It is part of the special education teacher's responsibility to make sure that SDI is a natural part of the learning environment in a co-taught classroom. SDI is part of the logical and legal process of making sure that a student's

IEP and individualized needs are being met as they access the general education curriculum. SDI is what makes the role of the special education teacher in the inclusive setting valuable and necessary. There will be students who need more supports beyond what the universal scaffolds offer.

SUPPORTING THE RANGE OF VARIABILITY THROUGH SDI

Let's consider a scenario where two co-teachers create an accessible learning environment for learners to read, comprehend, and express their understanding of the content. Now, let's zoom in on three students in that class who have weak decoding, comprehension, writing, and organizational skills. The selected co-teaching model(s) serve to remove important barriers that are good for all learners. For example, having the text read to them through options of multimedia and teacher supports will guide and engage the students' comprehension skills. The options for expressing their comprehension through writing are supported by allowing them to sketch and speak with peer collaborations. Yet, students with more intensive needs require further supports—such as direct instruction for decoding, additional teacher modeling, and systematic practice with comprehension and writing as well as a task analysis approach to organizing the steps needed to complete assignments. This is the purpose of the inclusive setting. One of the main purposes of having a special education teacher in the room is so that SDI will be a natural part of the learning process, and so that further supports and interventions will be included beyond the UDL scaffolds that help all learners. So, let's put this together:

- Co-teaching models provide the structure to organize learning, but these models alone do not create meaningful learning. These models are the outer shell that supports the potential for powerful learning to occur.

- UDL principles, guidelines, and strategies provide educators with options for elevating instruction. They are the strategies and scaffolds that create a clear, meaningful pathway so that all learners can connect within the moments of instructional time.

- Specially designed instruction must come into play when co-teachers are designing instruction and planning for those students who require further supports and interventions as outlined on their IEPs. SDI must be evident in all co-taught classrooms. If it is not present, then why have the special education teacher assigned to the class in the first place?

Continuing with our example, as we focus on the three students who need additional supports, the co-teachers must make time to provide explicit instruction in decoding, comprehension, writing, and organization. This can be done within the structure of this lesson. Since the students are in small groups, teachers may have the flexibility to work more explicitly with some students. In addition, these teachers must be mindful to incorporate these strategic and explicit supports on a regular basis. A UDL mindset and the co-teaching models create this flexibility and lower the number of barriers that these students have to contend with during any given lesson. In addition, ongoing communication between the general education and special education teacher will ensure a smooth flow to the process of learning.

So far, we have discussed the value of implementing a variety of co-teaching models to structure the learning in an inclusive, co-taught classroom. In addition, embracing a UDL mindset is the next layer to ensuring that the instruction within the selected co-teaching models is designed to create access and meaningful learning for each learner. Let's move along to a necessary update in our thinking about differentiation and UDL as a means of elevating our teaching and learning practices.

ALIGNING WITH DIFFERENTIATION AND POWERING UP WITH THE UDL GUIDELINES

One of the main updates in this second edition is to finally clear up confusions around differentiated instruction (DI) and UDL. In the spirit of a UDL process, I have learned so much since writing the first edition about how to express a clear understanding about how UDL and DI coexist. This edition shares a way to explain DI and the UDL Guidelines that moves beyond the tendency of comparing and contrasting the two conceptual structures around unnecessary and often inaccurate "either/or" consequences. Expressions like "fixing the student," "proactive," and "retroactive" have been used to describe the differences between the two (I even used this language in the first edition). Yet these very terms, though well intentioned, seem to create more confusion, frustration, and misconceptions. This edition holds the same beliefs as the first edition. However, I go further into the layers of our understanding with a focus on reconsidering the language we all use to try to make sense of meaningful and effective instructional practices. DI was always meant to be proactive. Like UDL, it was always meant to meet the students at their current place of understanding. And finally, it was never intended to be understood as a concept that indicated a human to be broken—hence "fixing the student." So, all these years after writing the first edition, I still grapple with how the world perceives DI and UDL. Once upon a time, I, too, fell into the spin of believing one to be proactive while the other is retroactive. Yet, both UDL and DI share too many commonalities to keep up the confusion that often results in trying to define them in binary ways. My understanding holds the belief that the language we use makes all the difference. The language of struggling learners, "high-low" students, and so forth just seems to keep a deficit-minded view. When we replace labeling students in such a way and embrace learners as variable instead—well, then, we have shifted the lens from this retroactive feel to a strong proactive lens. So, let's clear the air and unite two powerful teaching and learning structures.

▶ Differentiated Instruction and UDL: A Unified View

Differentiated instruction (Tomlinson, 1999) is one of the techniques frequently applied within the process of effective SDI. Differentiation is also a natural part of the UDL process. Educators know that in order to make learning meaningful, students must attach personal connections to ensure motivation and retention. Therefore, educators must consider students' needs, interests, and abilities. Tomlinson (1999) suggests that in order to create effective classroom environments, teachers must differentiate lessons and activities to support learners' various levels of readiness, interests, and learning profiles. Teachers accommodate and make instructional decisions that support individual student needs. Students are provided choices to make the learning process authentic and meaningful to each learner. So far this feels like designing with UDL in mind, right?

In a UDL classroom, differentiating instruction is embedded into the planning, implementation, and assessment of student achievements. All too often, teachers become overwhelmed at the mere thought of differentiating instruction. The pacing of instruction, coupled with the varying levels of students' abilities, often results in teachers claiming they do not have time to differentiate. That is because teachers' perception of differentiating instruction places a focus on the perceived categories of learners (high, low, struggling, exceling, etc.) and the areas (aka deficits) individual students need support in to be successful in the lesson. Yet there is a way to make differentiating instruction a natural part of the planning and learning process.

When we approach the idea of differentiating instruction, we will be successful as we look through a UDL lens. That is, we embrace the variability of the learners in any classroom—not viewing students as types of learners or deficits as a result of a categorized disability. Teachers must be mindful of their perceptions of students with disabilities. Traditionally, what happens far too often is that teachers start planning with the student's disability in mind and then they go about fitting structures and strategies to support specific deficits in the student's learning profile. When differentiating through a UDL lens, the teacher focuses on the variability of all learners. Let's look at an example.

DIFFERENTIATION WITH AN UNINTENDED (YET COMMON) DEFICIT-MODEL VIEW	DIFFERENTIATION WITH UDL MINDSET
The focus tends to be on the student's "struggles" and area of "disability."	A teacher who differentiates instruction through a UDL lens first looks at the barriers in the environment and the curriculum. For instance, it is not Gregory's weakness in decoding that is the barrier—it is, for example, a) the level of the text, and b) the expectation that students are to read silently and independently at their seats.
These teachers go about trying to apply strategies to support specific deficits in a student's learning profile. For example, if Gregory has a weakness in decoding, the teachers may support by saying, "How can we make it so Gregory can decode this text? How can we increase his decoding ability so he can learn alongside his peers?"	
In this example, designing instruction is through the lens of first identifying Gregory's deficit in decoding. The focus is on Gregory's weakness and the teachers' valiant efforts to erase the weakness.	The focus on variability embraces the notion that Gregory, and every learner in the room, falls within the natural range of abilities that occurs in any classroom. That is, all learners perceive, engage, express, and experience learning in personal ways.

DIFFERENTIATION WITH AN UNINTENDED (YET COMMON) DEFICIT-MODEL VIEW	DIFFERENTIATION WITH UDL MINDSET
Yet frustration ensues because the pacing of the curriculum along with the level of complexity of the text just keeps a one- to two-year achievement gap in place as he continues through the grade levels each year. Differentiating alone—without an awareness of UDL—may unintentionally create a learning environment where teachers categorize their students through their learning style preferences, which often do not fit within the context of learning for a particular lesson.	The focus on variability has been described as a "proactive" approach. But what we have to understand is that differentiation is also meant to be a proactive approach. However, the focus when differentiating through the UDL lens is on variability and breaking down barriers in the environment. In the case of Gregory, as the teachers provide UDL scaffolds for all learners by including multimedia text-to-speech along with teacher- and peer-supported opportunities, the barriers that Gregory might face are anticipated and addressed before instruction even begins. Just-in-time supports are already available. More explicit decoding instruction (keeping SDI in mind) during other points in the day may be necessary to supplement these proactive strategies.

When teachers apply differentiation without a UDL perspective, the focus tends to be on the disability the student presents (hence, there is an unintentional "fixing the learner" feel to the planning and implementation process).

In addition, teachers' perceptions of applying DI alone may result in categorizing students into "high–low" or "strong–struggling" groups that may unintentionally marginalize students. When differentiating alone, teachers may easily end up reteaching because in the moments of class time, the focus was on having the students fit into a rigid curriculum. From a UDL perspective, the focus is on having the curriculum fit into the various needs of all learners. The UDL principles drive the conviction that all learners in any room are variable along the three brain networks, and there is never a need to categorize them into any other group. When teaching with a UDL mindset, teachers use variability as the lens, and the needs of all students are met through natural scaffolds and opportunities for them to take charge of their own learning; this can be true for the DI process as well, as long as variability is illuminated. UDL naturally embeds DI, and it is this unified awareness that empowers educators to co-create meaningful learning experiences with every learner in their class.

UDL and DI in the Classroom at a Glance

UDL	DI
Is proactive in considering learner variability and the three UDL principles that guide options for multiple learning pathways through student choice.	According to Sousa and Tomlinson (2018), DI is intended to be proactive. In theory, it is. Yet oftentimes it is the teachers' perceptions of how to reach students with disabilities that create a more reactive approach. Too many teachers plan for specific learning style options, or they focus first on the students' disabilities rather than variability and the three brain networks. Therefore, teacher application often provides options that may be too rigid and misaligned with students' learning strengths for the context of that lesson.
The focus is on identifying the barriers in the curriculum, so that all students may easily participate, learn, and express their understanding in ways that make sense to them. Variability of learners is embraced through the three brain networks that meet the strengths and needs of each learner.	In teacher application, the focus is often on identifying the strengths and needs in the student. Teachers start with their lesson plan and say, "How can I help this learner achieve this lesson's goals?" Learning style options are often provided, and the teacher then works to support the learner in achieving lesson objectives.
Choice is embedded in learner-centered ways. Students make choices in the way they process and express their knowledge and understanding. Oftentimes, students can be a part of creating choice options.	In teacher application, choice is embedded mainly by teachers providing options for students based on what they think is best for students.

When UDL is applied, all students have options to perceive, apply strategies, and express their understanding in ways that deepen their personal learning experiences. Learning preferences may change from lesson to lesson depending on the context. High expectations are set for all learners, and the process to achieve those high expectations is supported through natural scaffolds that work to guide learners to connect personally to the curriculum. In order for powerful learning environments to unfold, the co-teachers must develop a positive co-teaching relationship.

The bottom line is this: As we apply UDL, we are naturally embedding differentiated instruction. It is that simple. The line in the sand is so blurred that there is no need to see it through a binary lens. When educators need to ask, "What is the difference between DI and UDL?" The response, in my mind, should be clear: Let's focus on the array of commonalities and empower our use of DI and UDL by merging them rather than embracing a dualistic approach. When DI and UDL are implemented with integrity, there is no duality.

So, it is clear that DI is a natural part of UDL. Now how can we include UDL as a natural part of DI? The short answer is . . . we already do! DI plans for teachers to differentiate through content, process, product, and affect and environment (Sousa & Tomlinson, 2018). Within the differentiation process, the three UDL principles can guide teachers in embracing variability rather than viewing students within categorized groups. In addition, the process of providing choice for all learners will become well organized and automatic over time with the three brain networks as a consistent, manageable guide.

But what happens with students who need more support? These are the variable learners in our room with IEPs who require more explicit instruction with additional supports. As we have discussed, UDL is a way to design instruction to make sure that any unintentional instructional and learning barriers are taken away from the beginning. When UDL is considered, teachers create a more accessible learning environment that increases the opportunities for learners to meaningfully interact with the material, participate in the process of learning, and gain personal academic and social skills that lead to deeper understandings.

For example, let's consider this scenario. The learning goal in this inclusive classroom requires students to demonstrate their comprehension of a text by writing a summary paragraph. Through the UDL lens, the co-teachers consider that the skills require students to demonstrate decoding, fluency, comprehension, knowledge of vocabulary, and written expression. The teachers know they have students who struggle with these tasks. The teachers then consider the co-teaching models and decide which structure(s) would help to create access. They look at the UDL Guidelines to guide the types of scaffolds they could provide for specific student needs. They also know they do not have a lot of time to prepare this lesson.

Here's how it could play out:

- Considering multiple means of engagement, the teachers decide to increase student interest by providing choices. They offer three options for a first reading of the text. The students may read the text silently, listen to the text using headphones and visual and audio supports on Chromebooks, or read the text in a shared reading group with one of the teachers.

- Considering multiple means of representation, the teachers explore options for perception by providing a vocabulary list written on chart paper with definitions, as well as vocabulary supports through use of a dictionary/thesaurus app. The text will be offered via multimedia through Chromebooks. Teachers will facilitate comprehension by providing feedback, modeling the process of visualization through a think-aloud approach, and modeling decoding and fluency.

- Considering multiple means of action and expression, the teachers decide to vary their methods of response. They know that, eventually, each student must provide a written summary paragraph. However, they know that a few students need some scaffolding to support the organization of their thoughts. The teachers again decide to allow students to illustrate their ideas by sketching key ideas and then writing a caption to describe their sketch. (This caption and sketch will be used to support their writing of the paragraph in the near future.) Students also have the option to work with a peer, where one peer will speak and the other peer will write what the other has said. The peers then switch roles, so that both students have the opportunity to speak and write—yet it is a collaborative process that guides deeper understandings.

Both teachers are happy with the ideas for supporting students' skill sets. They decide that the team-teaching co-teaching model will be best for opening the lesson. They then move to student choice groups (a modified version of station teaching) and provide one-to-one assistance and small-group instruction as needed. During the opening of the lesson and team-teaching approach, one teacher engages the class in a review of active reading strategies. The other teacher takes over by previewing the vocabulary words through class discussion and use of the visual chart. Both teachers add their thoughts along the way. It is a quick 15-minute opening that creates the support, structure, and engagement for *each* learner in the room to connect with the lesson.

It was a lesson that did not take a lot of time to plan and prepare—the co-teaching models and the UDL scaffolds were naturally embedded in a way to focus on the learning goals. The UDL scaffolds, along with the structure of their specifically selected co-teaching models, "fixed" the curriculum by providing an accessible process of learning for each student. Students with and without IEPs were given the supports they needed to meaningfully participate in the learning.

Creating lessons and units for any classroom becomes a positive experience with a UDL mindset. However, there is additional value and necessity in applying the process of UDL with inclusive classrooms where learner variability clearly spans a wide spectrum of abilities. Educators fall into natural planning and instructional routines where they proactively plan in ways that consider how the three UDL principles align with students' needs and ability to connect to material. In addition, a UDL mindset becomes natural in the moments of instruction because teachers are flexible in meeting the needs of students during the actual learning moments.

For example, consider a teacher who plans for students to gain important social studies content through the use of visuals such as a SMART Board presentation and whole-class discussion. As the lesson unfolds, the teacher realizes that this visual modality is not enough and decides within the moments of the lesson to allow students to further investigate the material through cooperative learning discussions and use of iPads so that they can explore the topic through their own research. Using proactive planning and additional learning pathways helps this teacher plan for realistic learner variability rather than singling out (or even worse, ignoring!) those students in the margins.

I shudder to think for a moment about the teacher who muddles through the SMART Board lesson with the whole-class discussion where students' learning needs are not met. What happens next? Well, we know the story . . . students become disengaged and disenchanted, and over time do not demonstrate their true capabilities as learners. Educators with a UDL mindset believe that students achieve their personal best when lessons are proactively planned for all learners in mind. Let's erase the margins and create true inclusive settings!

So how do we get the content, high expectations, learning targets, skills, and strategies across to our students? We know it's not simply a matter of providing the lecture or the visuals and, voilà, students have gained the knowledge and skills of all we intended to teach. Effective teaching is much deeper than that. Scaffolding the instruction is the golden ticket that teachers can provide to students in the inclusive classroom. It is their opportunity to become active learners who gain knowledge, skills, and strategies through learning processes. When taught well, these strategies will become a part of the student's repertoire of learning tools to guide them to be an independent learner. In one of his famous talks on teaching and creativity, Sir Ken Robinson states that teaching is an art form. His words make me feel like he is right here in the conversation with us:

> *That's why I always say that teaching is an art form. It's not a delivery system. I don't know when we started confusing teaching with FedEx. Teaching is an arts practice. It's about connoisseurship and judgment and intuition. We all remember the great teachers in our lives. The ones who kind of woke us up and that we're still thinking about because they said something to us or they gave us an angle on something that we've never forgotten. (Robinson & Aronica, 2014)*

SCAFFOLDS, SCAFFOLDS, SCAFFOLDS

The scaffolds we create become the tools of our artistic creations. In the UDL classroom, teachers create learning environments where a student's classifications are not used as a way of defining who they are as a learner. When teachers create UDL environments, all students value their thinking and their learning process, and embrace the process it takes to gain and retain knowledge. As I mentioned earlier, the UDL Guidelines provide specific ideas for naturally incorporating strategies to scaffold students' learning to make the process as meaningful as possible.

As Chapter 4 noted, we have psychologist Lev Vygotsky to thank for the concept of scaffolding the learning for our students. In fact, Vygotsky's work (1978) naturally supports CAST's framework for the three brain networks (recognition, strategic, and affective) that we discussed earlier in this book. Vygotsky suggested through his research that each learner has a zone of proximal development (ZPD)—that is, the sweet spot where learners are challenged and, with a little support, can learn even more. At the lower level of the zone, a learner can reach certain levels on their own; with additional assistance, they can achieve challenging tasks without getting too frustrated. When assistance is provided with the appropriate level of scaffolds, the learner could become independent and reach higher levels of thinking and performance. Those scaffolds can then be gradually released as the learner grows in skill or knowledge. It is within that opportunity for learning with assistance and scaffolds that learners push beyond limitations or barriers. These learning opportunities begin when educators recognize the present levels of performance (the learner's zone of actual development) and then scaffold the learning to guide deeper learning and greater independence in time (Vygotsky, 1978).

Within Vygotsky's "I Do, We Do, You Do" scaffolded structure, learners are actively engaged in a process of learning toward independence. During a cycle of instruction, students proceed along a series of steps that begins with an explicit modeling by the teacher(s) to provide full disclosure of how to apply a particular skill or strategy ("I Do"). The teacher then engages in a relaxed "let's try this together" mindset, so students have the opportunity to begin to apply a skill or strategy, but with guidance as needed ("We Do"). Once this interactive phase is completed, the students are directed to practice on their own ("You Do"). The teacher(s) may provide options for students to work in pairs, in groups, or individually. The teacher(s) use this time to monitor students' progress and to guide independent application. Figure 6.2 illustrates this "I Do, We Do, You Do" model.

This scaffolded structure in Figure 6.2 provides the right balance of teacher support and student application. The learning process is naturally embedded with the right degree of challenge to keep students eager to apply their knowledge and skills on their way to becoming resourceful, strategic learners. When

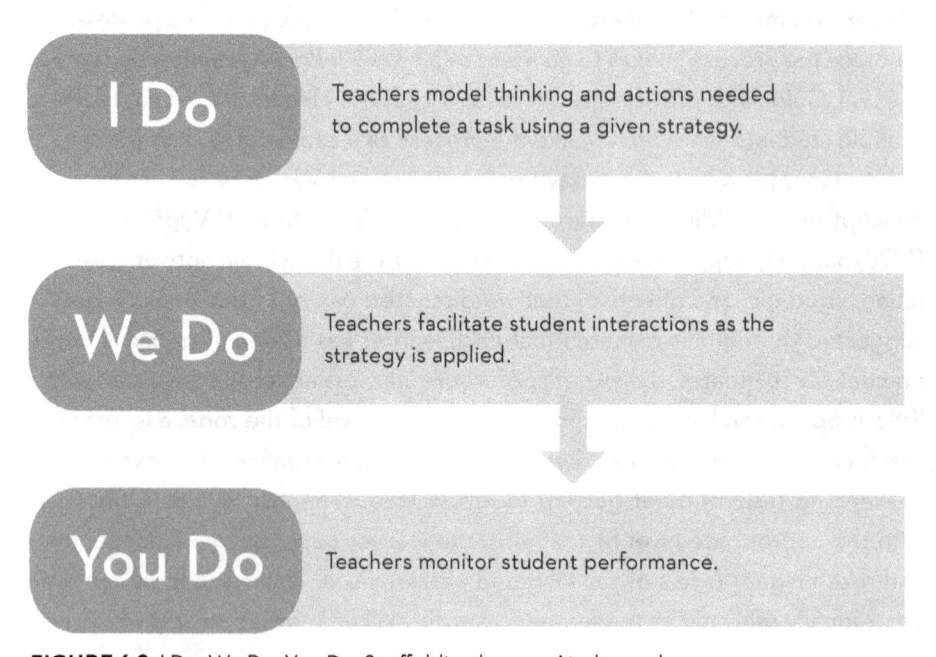

I Do	Teachers model thinking and actions needed to complete a task using a given strategy.
We Do	Teachers facilitate student interactions as the strategy is applied.
You Do	Teachers monitor student performance.

FIGURE 6.2. I Do, We Do, You Do: Scaffolding learners' independence

students are engaged in meaningful and challenging work, motivation to learn increases (Gargiulo & Metcalf, 2016). Let's take a look at an example of scaffolding efficiently for variable learners.

▶ General Tips for Effective Scaffolding

1. Identify what the students need to know and be able to do.

   Consider the lesson you will be teaching and decide on the background students will need to know. Identify any barriers between students' current performance levels and the desired achievement.

2. Begin with students' abilities.

   Create learning experiences that balance students' feeling successful and feeling motivated to complete more complex tasks.

3. Guide students in a frustration-free style.

   Keep the learning target in mind and provide scaffolds toward achieving that target. For example, if the learning target is to have students gain and express knowledge of historical facts and write an essay, provide opportunities for learning along the way. For instance, incorporate opportunities that represent the material through multimedia formats to give students additional examples to perceive the information. In addition, create space for students to engage in discussions, and/or choice to sketch ideas or jot ideas in an outline format to express their understanding of the historical facts before they are expected to write the essay.

4. Create a true learning community.

   Individuality is honored and respected. Everyone has an opportunity to share their voice.

5. Monitor and celebrate small successes.

   Know when to nudge learners forward and when to release to see what they are able to do. Limit frustration and maximize success, and you will naturally motivate students to want to learn more.

6. Guide students to take charge of their learning.

   Gradually release responsibility to the students. Create natural self-monitoring opportunities. Maximize opportunities to learn and practice executive function skills and strategies throughout each day.

SCAFFOLDING FOR VARIABLE LEARNERS

Enter this sixth-grade science class . . .

As part of a unit on atmosphere and climate, the class was learning about cloud formation and types of clouds. My general education co-teaching partner, Ms. Fields, and I did not have any co-planning time, but she shared the content and the Microsoft PowerPoint visuals with me through email. As Ms. Fields entered the room, she and I welcomed the class, and then she launched the lesson through a class discussion supported by visual slides and a video presented on the SMART Board. I prepared a sheet of chart paper at the side of the room and was ready to model taking notes with a Cornell Note-Taking Outline (Figure 6.3).

The instructional routine was already established since the beginning of the school year, so students were ready to decide how they planned to take notes. Some chose their notebooks (blank sheets of paper), and others chose the graphic organizer provided by the teachers. As Ms. Fields engaged the students through visual slides and videos, I added to her thinking by extending an idea and by paraphrasing key ideas for clarification and deeper comprehension.

Throughout the lesson, I modeled a note-taking technique for additional visual supports and organization. Following a 20-minute visual and auditory introduction to the types of clouds, Mrs. Fields surprised everyone (including me!) and directed the students to use their class notes to write a paragraph answering the following questions:

- What are clouds and how do they form?
- Describe the four kinds of clouds.

I jumped into solution-seeking mode because I immediately thought about the three students in the class who struggled significantly with writing.

As the students reviewed their notes, I quietly suggested to Ms. Fields that we provide a few minutes for students to collaborate prior to their actual writing time. She was hesitant because she wanted this to be an independent assessment, but she trusted my instincts—and she knew that the actual writing time would still be the students' independent work. I then instructed the students to move their desks into groups of four. I informed them that they had five minutes to discuss their thinking with one another before writing their individual paragraphs.

Cornell Notes Sheet

Name: _____   Date: _____

Topic: _____   Text: _____

Key Words, Phrases, or Questions	Notes

Summary: Write 5–8 sentences to sum up your learning from these notes.

FIGURE 6.3. Cornell Note-Taking Outline

While students collaborated, I went over to Jason. He struggled with written expression but had a strong background knowledge base. In addition, I knew that Jason played the guitar and enjoyed creating songs. With a sticky note and pencil in hand, I sat with Jason and his group. After reading the comprehension questions, I asked the group: "What would a song about describing clouds sound like?" All of the students sat up a bit taller—all smiling. One said, "I have no idea!" Another student just began to sing the questions out loud. And then Jason chimed in, "Oh, that's easy . . ." And he began to whisper his song.

As he began to sing a few lyrics of his newly created "cloud song," the other kids in the group began to tap on their desks to provide some rhythm and cheer him on. Through this quiet excitement, I wrote some of the keywords from Jason's song on a sticky note. After the two-minute song, the entire class clapped in honor of Jason's creativity. I then put the sticky note on Jason's desk and began to walk to another group. Jason and I exchanged a smile as he took the note and began to put his keywords into his best paragraph writing. He was engaged!

Following this cooperative group discussion time, Eric, another student who struggled with writing, was able to compose a paragraph with his best efforts because the time with peers served to engage and empower his abilities. I needed to touch base with one more student in the class. Michael needed further support. He sat quietly and proudly as the rest of the class finished their writing.

He said he was done. Figure 6.4 shows his finished, independently written paragraph.

> they're more than pretty fun shapes in the sky but it's actually weather.

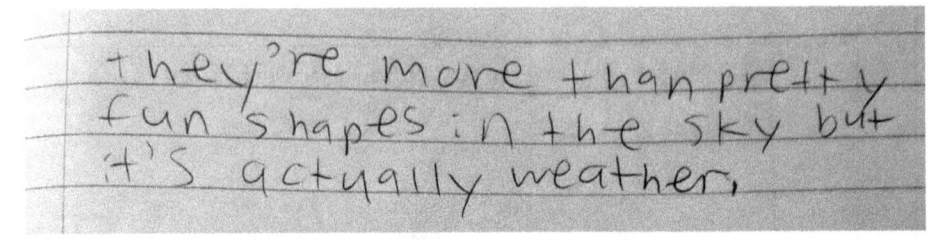

FIGURE 6.4. Michael's first effort

I acknowledged his efforts for executing this great beginning, but I let him know that I knew he had more to say. I guided him—on the spot—to add more details to his thinking by using the Question–Answer–Details (QAD) strategy. I did not have time to get fancy, so I took out a sheet of loose-leaf paper and provided him with a three-column visual to scaffold his thinking. He remembered learning this strategy with me earlier in the year in our study skills class period.

Once I quickly wrote the template, Michael immediately got to work. He first wrote the question, *What are clouds?* He wrote his answer, as seen on his first attempt in paragraph writing, Figure 6.4. *They're more than fun shapes in the sky.* And then he looked at me. I responded to his nonverbal inquiry by asking him, "What do you have to do next?" He responded, "Add details." I smiled and stayed quiet. He looked at his notes and then added, *They're made of tiny water droplets or ice crystals.* I said, "Now go back to your question—do you think your answer and detail answer the question?" He said, "Yes." I said, "Then keep going!" I gave him a thumbs-up and walked away. He continued to use the QAD strategy to guide his thinking to go deeper (Figure 6.5).

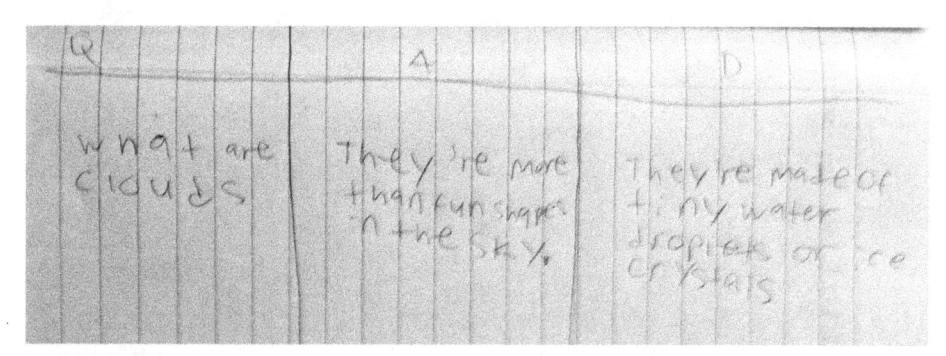

FIGURE 6.5. Michael adds detail

Class time ended and Michael had not yet finished his paragraph. But he was engaged! This strategy guided him to organize his thoughts on paper as a scaffold to writing the paragraph on a blank sheet of paper. He asked for a pass to come back at lunch to finish writing his paragraph. His final paragraph (Figure 6.6) was completed in 15 minutes.

The power of co-teaching is highlighted in this example on so many levels. For starters, rather than spinning our wheels about not having consistent co-planning time, my co-teacher and I combined our efforts by remaining flexible in the moment. In this particular lesson, Ms. Fields presented the material in multiple ways through options of perception (visual and auditory). I added further visual supports and strategic thinking by modeling a note-taking technique using a strategy that was previously taught to the class. In her last-minute decision to embed a formative assessment writing sample, Ms. Fields did not stop to think that three students in the class would need additional supports. But with the power of two teachers in the room, this was not a problem. Ms. Fields trusted in our various modes of expertise as well as in our co-teaching process.

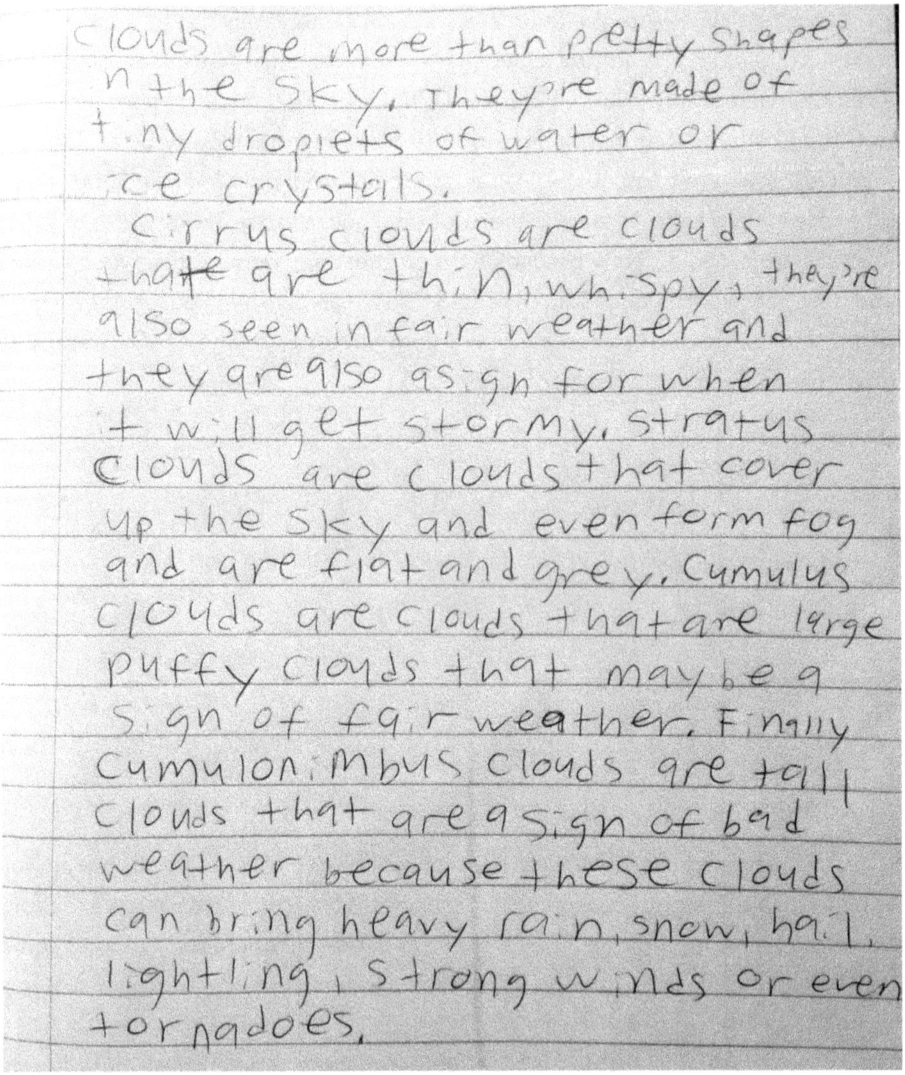

> Clouds are more than pretty shapes n the sky. They're made of tiny droplets of water or ice crystals.
> Cirrus clouds are clouds that are thin, whispy, they're also seen in fair weather and they are also a sign for when it will get stormy. Stratus clouds are clouds that cover up the sky and even form fog and are flat and grey. Cumulus clouds are clouds that are large puffy clouds that may be a sign of fair weather. Finally Cumulonimbus clouds are tall clouds that are a sign of bad weather because these clouds can bring heavy rain, snow, hail, lightling, strong winds or even tornadoes.

FIGURE 6.6. Michael's final paragraph

Ms. Fields was flexible to go with my lead to continue guiding all learners, while including additional specialized supports to a few students. Not only does cooperative learning work very well to allow students to take charge of their own learning, but it also gives teachers time to support individuals and small groups as needed. This example demonstrates how co-teachers can forge a bond of collaboration and flexibility as they trust each other's instincts and expertise within the real-time instructional moments.

▶ Multiple Means of Co-teaching Effectiveness

Engagement

- Provide ongoing personal and collaborative opportunities to optimize the motivation to co-teach. When teachers focus on the goals of the students and of the curriculum, they maintain a clear focus.

- Include mastery-oriented feedback. Co-teachers should be transparent with one another. Share your thoughts to allow for open, honest collaborations.

- Provide opportunities for each teacher to share their choice of instructional methodologies and routines. Value one another's opinions and perspectives.

- Create a co-teaching check-in process to assess your own co-teaching practices.

- Complete a Class Learning Profile (see Chapter 5) and apply the Strengths-Based Inventory (see Chapter 5) for a quick reflective process that can increase communication and coping skills to keep the co-teaching relationship moving in positive directions.

Representation

- Make sure you both have a clear understanding of the varied co-teaching models.

- Communicate through discussions in person, email, Google Docs, sticky notes, and so forth to maximize ideas for promoting instructional content and processes.

Action and Expression

- Set goals for your co-planning and for your instructional processes. A weekly basis for goal-setting will keep the goals reasonable and meaningful.

- Share strategies to support various pathways of learning along with supporting each other's expertise.

- Use a check-in process to monitor the effectiveness of your instructional planning and implementations.

✔ Co-teaching Check-In Activity

Three Words

Use three words that describe how you are feeling about your co-teaching experience. Consider share words that describe how you are feeling about your role during planning and instructional time. Invite a brief conversation to describe why you selected these words; perhaps there is a story to go with one or more of the adjectives. Respond to each other's selection. Perhaps you can provide an example to support one or more of the adjectives your co-teacher self-selected. Have fun and let the conversation unfold!

Advancing into the relationship version: Each co-teacher selects three adjectives to describe their co-teacher from what they know at the point of participating in this activity. Be honest. Be humble. Be transparent to share how you perceive your co-teacher—and let the candid conversations unfold. There is nothing like embracing the perspective of others as we get to know ourselves.

KEY TAKEAWAYS

✔ SDI is explicit, systematic instruction that meets the students where they are and guides them to strengthen their skills and knowledge base.

✔ SDI is part of the logical and legal process of making sure that a student's individualized needs are being met as they access the general education curriculum.

✔ Co-teaching models provide an external structure to organize learning, and the UDL principles and guidelines provide options for designing accessibility and meaningful instruction within the structure.

✔ There is no reason to dichotomize UDL and DI. UDL naturally embeds DI. It is through this unified lens that educators may be empowered to co-create meaningful learning experiences with their students.

✔ Scaffolding instruction provides a harmonious balance of teacher supports and student voice and application.

✔ Weaving UDL within the instructional process while varying the application of co-teaching models is a way to reach the variable learners that make up any inclusive setting.

✔ When differentiation is applied without a UDL lens, the focus is on "fixing" the learner—which is why it can feel like a daunting task. When differentiation is applied through a UDL lens, the focus is on fixing the curriculum (not on fixing the student). The instruction is designed with scaffolds in place to support the natural variability of all learners.

✔ UDL fosters personal and academic growth as each learner experiences the effects of becoming an expert learner (achieving their absolute personal best). Variable teaching styles and areas of teacher expertise are applied through the co-teaching models and through strategic best practice.

✔ Designing instruction with UDL strategies removes many instructional barriers and creates an accessible learning environment with opportunities for meaningful deeper learning activities. Some students in an inclusive classroom will require further supports through the special education teacher's expertise and application of specially designed instruction.

✔ Co-plan to implement UDL strategies for all students by providing scaffolds and strategies to support the three brain networks, and make sure to add specially designed instructional strategies to further support students who require additional scaffolds.

STUDY GROUP QUESTIONS

1. Think of one student in your class and discuss how SDI is implemented to connect their IEP goals with one specific lesson and with the general education curriculum in general.

2. Your colleagues tell you they are not sure that they are embedding SDI within their co-taught instruction. Furthermore, they state that they work hard to "stay at the pace of their grade-level colleagues." How would you respond to guide their understanding of the necessity, value, and process of including SDI in their daily instruction?

3. Think about a recent lesson and explain how your selected co-teaching model served as an external structure for the strategies you designed for that lesson. How did UDL show up within your design?

4. This second edition aims to present UDL and DI as a unified process of designing instruction. Explain your understanding of blending these powerful ways of co-creating meaningful learning in your classroom.

5. What are examples of recent scaffolds you included in your instructional design? Describe the balance of teacher support and students' actions along the application process.

7

Empowering Students as UDL Partners

ONE OF THE most powerful aspects of using the UDL Guidelines is the way they connect us to learners in the classroom. As we include specific strategies to guide strategic, goal-oriented learners, we automatically engage learners by promoting high expectations and self-empowerment. In addition, as we weave in multiple means of action and expression, we touch upon multiple ways of representing materials to meet the needs of the variability in our classrooms.

The strategies shared in this book may elevate the instructional process as two teachers join forces to make meaningful learning happen. Learners who are purposeful and resourceful know where to seek resources, and whom they can go to with questions and comments to seek more information. They become motivated and knowledgeable by setting goals and applying strategies that guide their thinking and confidence to be the absolute best version of themselves possible.

Just as we prepare students to embrace two teachers in the room as a positive aspect to their learning process, we must also naturally embed their abilities to embrace a UDL mindset. Let's start out here with a favorite quote that I like to share with students:

> *We have work to do. You can't just sit in a seat and grow smart. Promise, you are going to do, and you are going to produce. And I am not going to let you fail.* —MARVA COLLINS (1982), teacher, leader, and activist

From the beginning of our learning days together, students know that learning is an active process—it is a personal, emotion-filled learning process. And I, as their teacher, will do all I can to support, guide, and nudge them forward in positive ways to embrace themselves as learners. Failure is a positive aspect within a successful learning process, and students must embrace that their efforts and learning decisions are fueled by persistence and resiliency. I incorporate the words of Abdul Kalam to prepare students to allow positive learning energy to flow naturally throughout the school year:

> *If you fail, never give up because F.A.I.L. means "First Attempt In Learning." End is not the end, in fact E.N.D. means "Effort Never Dies." If you get No as an answer, remember N.O. means "Next Opportunity." So let's be positive.* —ABDUL KALAM, author, scientist, former president of India (Kalam & Tiwari, 1999)

Once the tone is set and this growth mindset view is embraced, students are ready to see that learning is an active process incorporating the multiple means of engagement, representation, and action and expression. Table 7.1 depicts how I share my UDL view as I launch a class discussion to hear students' connections, questions, and ideas.

TABLE 7.1. Introducing Students to UDL

MULTIPLE MEANS OF ENGAGEMENT	MULTIPLE MEANS OF REPRESENTATION	MULTIPLE MEANS OF ACTION AND EXPRESSION
Each of you will have opportunities to connect with what we learn. You will be a part of setting personal and group learning goals that will guide our plan of action for learning. You will participate in a variety of activities that will create opportunities for you not only to be inspired but to also inspire others. Each of you will have the opportunity to take charge of your own learning.	We will do our best to offer all material in a variety of ways. Sometimes visuals such as graphic organizers, maps, or videos will help you to learn something deeper. You will also have the opportunity to tell us if you need to see a topic or idea in another way.	Each learner in the room has unique talents and abilities. You will have many opportunities to collaborate with one another. Other times, you will be given the opportunity to work solo—to guide you to make sense of the material. Throughout the year you will have a variety of opportunities to express what you know about the topics we study. There will be opportunities to speak, write, create multimedia products, act out, sketch, and tap into our natural abilities to communicate our love of learning.

Reading picture books aloud is another effective way to relax and guide learners to connect to a specific concept you are teaching. In the case of UDL, two picture books by Peter Reynolds are a perfect way to introduce the idea of UDL to students in any grade:

- *The North Star* (Reynolds, 2009) is a book that expresses the fact that every individual is on a journey (and learning path) and requires different opportunities and decisions along the way to achieve personal success.
- *Ish* (Reynolds, 2004) shares a beautiful story of the value and necessity that struggling along one's learning path holds for true personal success to happen. It guides learners to value the creative side of action and expression, along with adopting a growth mindset along the way.

These stories could launch meaningful class discussion in how the UDL will be a natural part of the learning process in your classroom.

SUPPORTING ENGAGEMENT

As co-teachers, we want to create a relaxed learning environment that eliminates threats and distractions. The learning place is a comfortable one where each learner can share their thinking and listen to one another's thinking. Engaged learners feel a sense of independence as their level of confidence builds. They do not panic when they do not know something, but rather they are motivated by the challenge to seek answers. They know they are in a class that provides the structure and the strategies to guide their autonomy. They are active listeners because they do not feel the anxiety of being called on out of the blue. And if they are called on, they feel comfortable taking a risk and sharing out loud. They are relaxed enough to connect with the learning so they may gain the knowledge and strategic thinking needed to apply in all learning situations—not just for the moments of that class.

Picture this: You arrange your desks in pairs, in small groups of four, or in rows. You decide the arrangement of the desks depending on your lesson. You make certain to keep the movement of furniture easy and natural. You and your co-teacher (any co-teacher) are on the move as you work in tandem to engage students with the process of learning. The two of you have conversations as you model the thinking and actions needed in a given learning situation. You also make time for learners to have conversations with one another as they process, solve, and push through challenges to complete academic tasks.

Other times, students are quietly working at their seats as they individually apply strategies to deeply connect with the materials and content. You and your co-teacher share the responsibility of representing the content with a keen sense of promoting strategic learners through a mindful emphasis on the process. An objective observer may be able to tell that one teacher is taking charge of teaching the content, and the other teacher is zooming in to teach the steps for strategic thinking. Yet this observer may not know which is the general education teacher and which is the special education teacher because they are both flexible in shifting the roles and responsibilities depending on the context of the lesson. The classroom is noisy in a purposeful manner. You hear students thinking out loud. You hear teachers guiding students' thoughts through effective questioning that deepens their engagement along the learning process. You hear students saying comments like, "Is class over already? That went fast!" Students in this class are accustomed to daily opportunities to meaningfully process information and make informed decisions.

One year as I launched a UDL-friendly environment at the beginning of the year with my fifth-grade co-teacher, we gave students a quick writing warm-up exercise. Students were given a few minutes to select a topic, and then had five minutes to write about their selected topic. One student sat quietly at his desk without writing. When I went over to check with him, he told me, "I've just never been given the choice before. I am usually forced to just write about a topic that a teacher tells me to write about. It's not easy to think about a topic." Since I knew this student's interests, I was able to take the time to weave a few questions to guide his focus. He selected a topic and began to write.

The seeds of engagement were planted with those simple steps. A UDL classroom provides a rich learning environment where making decisions and sharing one's voice is within one's natural comfort zone of learning. The flow of a co-taught UDL classroom is smooth and relaxed. It includes ongoing planning and sharing, communication, learning process, assessment, and reflection. It is a process where each learner (including the teachers) has opportunities to think, share their voice, and value their thinking as well as the perspective of others in the room.

One of the most important teaching responsibilities is the necessity to guide students to actively monitor and regulate their learning process. The idea of self-regulation refers to the degree to which students can regulate the process of their thinking, motivation, and learning behaviors (Pintrich & Zusho, 2002). The following are six phases of the learning process that learners need to monitor:

1. Setting goals
2. Identifying and applying strategies used to achieve those goals
3. Seeking and utilizing appropriate resources
4. Applying effort
5. Being receptive and responsive to external feedback
6. Creating the result and product produced from the learning

Teachers must be mindful to guide students to depend on their own instincts as they plan, implement, and monitor their learning. Co-teachers find additional value in this because students who have been accustomed to learning through their focus on a specific disability may easily adopt a "learned helplessness" attitude, which catapults them into falling into unproductive learning traps. These students must work harder to achieve learning goals. Unless the right strategies and supports are in place, these students may not gain the stamina to push through the additional challenges.

As co-teachers make self-regulation a strong learning focus, these students have the opportunity to develop positive learning behaviors as they work toward their personal best versions of becoming expert learners.

KEEPING EXPECTATIONS HIGH FOR EVERY LEARNER

We have talked about the need to truly believe that every student can learn and that it is our responsibility to provide the learning environment that makes that possible. Throughout history, students with disabilities were given fewer complex tasks or were given accommodations that modified the curriculum in ways that expected them to do less. Through neuroscience and educational research, we know that the variability of all learners can be supported through instruction that is strong with scaffolds to guide students to connect meaningfully with the content.

Renowned special education researcher Edwin Ellis (1997) talks of "watering up the curriculum"—that is, offering the scaffolds, supports, and accommodations that maintain high expectations for all learners rather than dumbing down the curriculum. As I show here, the nine goals Ellis outlines can provide additional checkpoints for teachers as they weave high expectations with UDL supports into their learning environments:

1. More emphasis on students constructing knowledge

    Teachers facilitate learning to allow students to seek information, process, and express their understandings. Students have opportunities to connect previously learned information with new information.

    The UDL Connection:
    Consider multiple means of action and expression. Offer multiple tools and strategy use. Vary the methods of response to allow each learner to connect and express their expanded knowledge in meaningful ways.

2. More depth, less superficial coverage

    Teachers deliver learning experiences that allow students to process and understand why ideas are important and how ideas connect. Teachers make time to experience learning with students rather than just covering the information based on what is written in their plan book or curriculum guide.

    The UDL Connection:
    Consider multiple means of representation to allow students to perceive information in welcoming, familiar, and exciting ways. Once students make that first meaningful step, move the lesson into an active process where they are actively thinking, speaking, sharing, and learning.

3. More emphasis on developing relational understanding and knowledge connections

    As a way to guide deeper understandings, teachers provide students with the opportunity to see how ideas and concepts are connected. Information is taught within a context of what a student knows to allow them to associate new learning with known information.

    The UDL Connection:
    Consider multiple means of engagement. How can you optimize relevance, value, and authenticity as you connect your goals, content, and materials with

the strengths and needs of your students? Be a keen observer so you may read and understand how to guide each learner. Guide learners through multiple means of action and expression to connect new learning with previously taught information.

4. More student elaboration

Include many opportunities for students to not only hear their own thoughts but also share their voice. Cooperative learning, such as think-pair-share, provides valuable processing time for students to gain deeper understandings as well as confidence in their abilities.

The UDL Connection:
Consider multiple means of action and expression as you support strategy development.

5. More emphasis on the redundancy of archetype concepts, patterns, and strategies

Teachers facilitate learning in ways that guide learners to see connections, repetition, and associations to guide their understanding and memory for important information. For example, students are taught themes of geography to guide their understanding when learning about ancient civilizations.

The UDL Connection:
Consider multiple means of representation as you introduce new ideas. Including visuals and multimedia options through multiple means of action and expression will get students to see and experience the connections and associations to guide deeper understanding and retention.

6. More reflection and risk-taking

Teachers incorporate time for students to think about how they feel about what they are learning. They experiment with strategies that guide their learning, and they are free to share their ideas within an environment where their thinking is valued.

The UDL Connection:
Consider multiple means of engagement to foster a collaborative learning community where students reflect and self-regulate the application of specific strategies.

7. More social support for achievement

   Create opportunities for learners to strengthen their own voice as they develop tolerance and understanding for the views of others. In inclusive classrooms, cooperative learning and peer interactions are ideal opportunities for all learners to take the lead in learning as well as learn from their peers.

   The UDL Connection:
   Consider multiple means of engagement as you nurture an environment where learners value their thinking and are comfortable sharing their voice with peers. As students share their views, they learn to value the perspective of their peers.

8. More emphasis on developing habits of mind, thinking skills, and learning strategies

   Learners have ongoing opportunities to develop a growth mindset as they push through challenges. In addition, they learn a variety of strategies to guide them to be successful.

   The UDL Connection:
   Consider multiple means of action and expression, along with engagement as learners set goals, plan, and apply strategies that optimize learning and self-reflection.

9. More emphasis on developing a sense of personal potency

   The individual thinking of variable learners is valued. Each learner is supported along a learning process that fosters interpersonal, intrapersonal, and academic success.

   The UDL Connection:
   Consider all three UDL principles. Multiple means of engagement will connect learners with goals and self-reflection. Multiple means of representation will allow each learner to maximize personal connections and transfer of material. Multiple means of action and expression will support strategic, goal-directed learners.

The better learners connect the content with their own background knowledge, the more they will learn and remember. Research shows that when instruction is rigorous and allows each learner to have the opportunity to connect meaningfully with the learning, they will meet with new levels of personal success. And that is the overall mission of UDL—to create expert learners.

YOUR STRATEGIES TO "WATER UP"

Ellis's model of "watering up the curriculum" can help ensure that co-teachers apply scaffolds and accommodations in ways that maintain high expectations for all learners. We know that the variability of all learners can be supported through instruction that has strong scaffolds to guide students to connect meaningfully with the content.

When connected to the UDL Guidelines, Ellis's nine goals provide additional guidance for teachers to involve learners as allies in implementing UDL. In addition, these nine goals connect seamlessly to the UDL principles and guidelines. I invite you to review the nine goals again and consider how they may empower you and your co-teacher as you apply your emerging UDL mindsets.

In the space following each goal, add your thoughts about how you and your co-teacher are working toward it. Find time to discuss how you both feel about how you are embedding each of these goals.

1. More emphasis on students constructing knowledge

2. More depth, less superficial coverage

3. More emphasis on developing relational understanding and knowledge connections

4. More student elaboration

　

5. More emphasis on the redundancy of archetype concepts, patterns, and strategies

　

6. More reflection and risk-taking

　

7. More social support for achievement

　

8. More emphasis on developing habits of mind, thinking skills, and learning strategies

9. More emphasis on developing a sense of personal potency

_____

_____

_____

Now it's discussion time! How are you and your co-teacher combining your expertise to meet these nine watering-up goals? What are you doing? What is your co-teacher doing? How are you supporting one another to share your individual skill sets and at the same time empower your students?

✔ Co-teaching Check-In Activity

Rose, Bud, Thorn

This brief but powerful exercise can capture relevant ideas that co-teachers must share to maintain ongoing, transparent communication—not to mention continue to cultivate a strong partnership. Here are the basic steps:

1. Each co-teacher sketches a tri-column notes page or sticky note.

2. In the left column, write one thing that is going well that you feel great about—this is your "rose."

3. In the middle column, write one challenge, or "thorn," you are experiencing that you could use more support with.

4. In the third column, write one thing that you look forward to each week, or a new idea that you would like to know more about and possibly try in class together. This is your "bud."

Pass your writing to each other to silently read and then discuss—or jump into a conversation right away by taking turns sharing and discussing the boundless possibilities for how you may support and elevate your co-teaching!

KEY TAKEAWAYS

✔ UDL can be easily embedded within your daily classroom routines, structures, instructional decisions, and overall attitude for learning.

✔ As UDL weaves its way through this natural process, learners not only want to learn but also know how to learn.

✔ Co-teachers can set the tone by making intentional decisions to incorporate time for students to embrace struggling as a natural part of the learning process.

✔ UDL empowers teachers to optimize opportunities for students to learn from mistakes and become motivated to improve and continue to learn and share ideas.

✔ As teachers expose students to the language of the UDL principles and planned activities, students experience the opportunity to self-regulate and to take charge of their personal learning process. Through specific discussions, activities, and lessons, students begin to deepen their awareness about who they are as learners. Remember, our goal as educators is to create expert learners. That means we must value the thinking and the learning process of each learner. Each learner must have the opportunity not only to access the curriculum but also to experience it in ways that deepen their relationship with learning.

✔ With two teachers in the room, co-teachers can maximize learning by incorporating the talents of both teachers through varied co-teaching models, UDL strategies, and specially designed instruction as needed. Maintain high expectations for all learners by incorporating the specific goals of watering up the curriculum to elevate student voice, choice, and engaged learning experiences.

STUDY GROUP QUESTIONS

1. Discuss the benefits of introducing the UDL principles to your students.

2. How do you connect with the idea of watering up the curriculum? Share a specific example from a recent or upcoming lesson.

3. What are the ways you invite your students as UDL partners in your room? How does this affect your aim to co-create an inclusive classroom community? Be as specific as possible.

8

Creative Structures:
Making Space for Strategic Learning

CURRICULUM, GOALS, LESSON plans, routines, co-teaching models, and even the UDL Guidelines all provide an external structure to guide our internal beliefs about what learning should look and feel like. This chapter takes all the structures discussed in this book and shares a deeper look into what learning experiences may feel like. I will share a lesson planning structure I call Planning Pages. This chapter also shares a variety of strategies that serve as examples for creatively making space for students to think as individuals as well as a collective classroom community.

The instructional cycle in a co-taught UDL classroom deploys the four components of curriculum (see Chapter 3) in ways that enhance learners' abilities to build knowledge (recognition networks), strategies and skills (strategic networks), and the motivation and stamina to learn (affective networks). As co-teachers put their lessons into action with the UDL principles in mind, they can create a masterful flow of meaningful learning opportunities for each student. In doing so, they show that they:

- Respect that each learner (including each teacher!) is an individual with personal perceptions and ways of thinking.

- Embrace the talents, personalities, and expertise of both teachers (and their students!).

- Foster active learning to make sure all learners (that means every individual!) have the opportunity to connect with the curriculum.

- Incorporate formative assessment as a barometer of students' understanding and performance.

As we consider co-planning and designing lesson plans, I must confess: I do not see the point to writing comprehensive, multipage lesson plans. Did I shock anyone? Think about it—it is just not realistic given the pace of a teacher's day to write, much less read, them. There are only two reasons for making the time to write out complete and comprehensive lesson plans. First, during teacher preparation programs, preservice teachers must receive explicit instruction in the components that explain the details of any lesson. There are many comprehensive lesson plan formats that each university adopts to guide soon-to-be teachers. It is crucial that preservice teachers embrace this comprehensive process because it serves as a graphic organizer to guide the depths of thinking teachers must engage in when designing lessons. It also becomes ingrained in their minds, so the process becomes second nature in time.

The second reason is when a teacher works with a principal who collects and requires such multipage lessons. This reason is rare. In my experience, most administrators prefer concise, to-the-point, comprehensive lessons to review. Seriously, who has time to read through a multipage plan? Therefore, I share with you my idea of Planning Prompts pages. This type of planning is quick to write, and it incorporates all of the components we learned in our teacher preparation days. It is also a very manageable, informative way to plan lessons in a manner that actually helps us in the moments of lively learning with our co-teacher and students.

PLANNING PROMPTS

Planning Prompts is a lesson plan outline that anchors the co-teachers to the essence of the learning goals and curriculum focus while at the same time creating space for the in-the-moment kind of learning that can never be planned ahead of time (although some of it may possibly be predicted as we get to know our students) because it comes from the students themselves as the moments of teaching and learning unfold. I developed this structure in the early stages of my teaching career when I was in survival mode. I was a special education teacher working with many different teachers in resource room and co-taught classroom settings, and I needed to find my footing. You will notice that my focus on differentiating instruction (I did not know about UDL yet—imagine that!) was front and center. A few years later as I began to embrace UDL, I realized that the process and product aspects of my outline provided the space for me to embed the UDL principles. See Figure 8.1 for an example of a sixth-grade social studies lesson.

Subject: English/Social Studies   **Topic of Lesson:** Ancient Egypt

Lesson Objective: Students will independently read S.S. text pages 70-73 and express their understanding using Key Notes note-taking.

Standards: Reading comprehension with text evidence to support thinking.

IEP Goals Addressed: 1. Increase comprehension in content-area reading. 2. Expand knowledge and application of content-area vocabulary. 3. Strengthen note-taking and study skills.

Essential Question: How does Key Notes help you when reading content-area texts?

Content: Ancient Egypt—pages 70-73 in text

(digital, hard copy, teacher model on board, classroom conversation)

Process: 10 min whole class—teachers model Key Notes (**Team Teaching—Speak and Add**)

(SMART Board content slides, document camera, teacher model on dry-erase board)

20 min small peer groups or solo (student choice) to read text (choice of hard copy, iPad digital copy, shared read with a teacher) (**Station Teaching, Workshop Model**)

10 min whole-class wrap-up—answer EQ (**Team Teaching**)

Product: Completed Key Notes page (handwritten or digital [student choice], and teacher anecdotal notes based on classroom conversations and observation of student performance)

Follow-Up Notes: Brett chose to go solo, worked well—needs more time to complete; Joseph chose shared read with teacher—needs to move toward more independent reading options (he is ready); Tricia and Paige chose to work with peers—they completed the Key Notes page in partnership, and then supported peers who needed guidance within their group.

© 2016 Elizabeth Stein

FIGURE 8.1. Planning Prompt example for a sixth-grade social studies lesson

Notice in Figure 8.1 that any lesson may be outlined quickly, and also—just as important—is visible at a glance, ensuring that teachers stay on track for achieving lesson goals and including student voice and choice along an organic learning experience. The Content, Process, Product structure is taken from the process of differentiating instruction. Planning Prompts also include UDL principles and co-teaching models within each section. The Content section shares not only the exact curriculum but also various ways material will be presented. The Process section shares the different ways the content will be scaffolded using multimedia and specific strategies. Finally, the Product section presents the options for formative assessment as a way to monitor students' understanding. The essential question (EQ) helps to keep the teachers on track for monitoring their own actions toward guiding students to achieve the lesson objective. The EQ launches the students' focus as the lesson begins and, if time permits, students may answer the EQ at the end of the lesson through dialogue or a brief written statement for teachers to gain insights into students' learning and teachers' next instructional decisions. Let's look at another example in Figure 8.2, this time in math. This lesson occurred as I coached a co-teaching pair to compromise and embrace each other's expertise.

Notice the way this lesson integrated UDL, differentiation, and co-teaching in an at-a-glance summary. It also guided the way both co-teachers participated in this classroom. The general education teacher typically taught each lesson as a whole class, followed by a 15-minute student application at their seats until the bell rang. The teacher would be available to answer questions and walk around; however, there were many students who just zoned out for the 15 minutes. They knew they would have more homework, but in that moment, they just weren't motivated to work through the last 15 minutes of class. Moreover, the special education co-teacher often felt like a silent visitor who supported students at their desks, if they raised their hands or she noticed someone needed help as she walked around. Restructuring the math lesson to incorporate the UDL principles and co-teaching models worked wonders to engage and support learners. The balance of whole class and small group—along with student choice throughout the process—served to keep the students active in thought and motivated by taking charge of their actions. There was choice in the ways they were supported, and no learner was singled out. The reteach and additional supports of review links and examples were available to everyone. The EQ kept an essential learning element at the forefront as teachers and students moved to the next class as the bell rang.

Subject: Math   **Topic of Lesson:** Percent Equations

Lesson Objective: Students will apply their knowledge of percent equations to real-life problems such as discount, tax, and tip.

Standards: Review with proportions in real-world application

IEP Goals Addressed: 1. Identify mathematical operations in context and accurately calculate.

All students need copies of class notes and additional examples provided in class.

Essential Question: Why is it important to know how to apply percent equations?

Content: District math curriculum—teacher made examples using teachers' names to share real-world stories as examples. Student names used to increase motivation and real-world applications as students apply. (Digital, hard copy, teacher modeling on board)

Process: 10 min whole class—activate background knowledge and introduce with own stories and model process **(Team Teaching—Speak and Add)**

(SMART Board content slides, document camera, teacher model on dry-erase board)

20 min small peer groups or solo (student choice) to complete math problems. Students have choice to review (teacher model on board, iPads with video link shared by teacher, reteach with teacher) **(Station Teaching, Workshop Model)**

10 min whole-class wrap-up—answer EQ **(Team Teaching)**

Product: Completed 3–5 real-world math problems, and teacher anecdotal notes based on classroom conversations and observation of student performance

Follow-Up Notes: JZ: Needed to stay in review longer, watched links on iPad with additional examples, began to apply. CM: Chose reteach group—attentive and active. GM: Chose solo, reviewed on own, asked peer next to him a question, began to work—so far, so good!

© 2016 Elizabeth Stein

FIGURE 8.2. Planning Prompt example for a seventh-grade math lesson

Let's look at another example of applying the Planning Prompt for powerful co-teaching and learning. This time, let's go to a seventh-grade science lesson I planned that incorporated a flipped learning experience.

FLIPPED LEARNING

Flipped learning is about embracing a keen focus on how best to use our in-person instructional time for those lessons that require a potential lecture or some other way of presenting content. Rather than spending in-person time presenting material to the whole class as students likely sit at their desks, take notes, and grasp the content, why not flip it? Provide students with the content through multimedia options on their own time. When they come to class, let the classroom conversations and applications begin! This experience provides options for meaningfully engaging learners through critical thinking, differentiating instruction, student choice, and active learning (Sams & Bergmann, 2013).

Deciding to Flip!

I decided to jump right in with this idea; however, it was a completely new concept for my co-teacher at the time. After I shared the basic idea, she was as enthusiastic as I was to give this flip a go! We decided on the topic of moon phases, since she said it was typically a topic that she presented in lecture style. I began to prepare for the lesson by asking myself four sequential questions:

1. What are our lesson objectives, and in what parts of the lesson would students need additional supports?
2. What tools, websites, or software will I use, and how can I set this up so all learners will have access to the information?
3. What concepts must the students know to be able to participate in the in-person class activities?
4. With limited to no planning time, how can I make sure we co-plan this lesson?

The Plan

I shared the plan (see Figure 8.3) with my co-teacher via Google Docs (this was pre–COVID pandemic, so this, too, was new for my co-teacher!). I shared various activities, and together, asynchronously, we made the final decisions for what would work best for our students. I knew there were six students in the class

Subject: Science/English **Topic of Lesson:** Moon Phases

Lesson Objective: Students will express their understanding of the phases of the moon through asynchronous multimedia options, guided note-taking, and in-class dialogue and lab activities.

Standards: Interpreting data and constructing explanations to describe the cyclic patterns of lunar phases.

IEP Goals Addressed: 1. Increase comprehension in content-area reading. 2. Expand knowledge and application of content-area vocabulary. 3. Strengthen note-taking and study skills. Apply specific strategies to guide ability to self-monitor learning.

Essential Question: Explain the importance of the moon phases? How did flipped learning help you as a learner?

Content: Flipped learning lesson with multimedia links and guided note-taking sheet

Process: Asynchronous: support student through email/phone calls as needed. Develop library access times for those who do not have access at home.

In class: Open conversation (**Team Teach**), Small group (You are the teacher) conversations and Lab work activity (**Station Teaching**)

Product: Completed guided notes (handwritten or digital [student choice], and teacher anecdotal notes based on classroom conversations and observation of student performance)

Follow-Up Notes: Billy: Impressive self-monitoring, opted to do all asynch activities, wrote additional information on his notes such as "I watched the video 3 times and then finally got this!" Julia: Active in class, applied academic vocab in group dialogues—typically quiet in class. Evan: Strong self-monitoring and guided notes, completed all work—typically missed homework assignments. "I am excited to check out the moon tonight to see what phase we are in." Motivated by self-paced, guided experience.

© 2016 Elizabeth Stein

FIGURE 8.3. Planning Prompt example for the seventh-grade flipped science lesson

who would need support with vocabulary as well as retaining the information. Therefore, I included vocabulary supports through flashcards via Quizlet (http://quizlet.com), and I created a guided notes sheet (Figure 8.4) to support active participation when viewing materials. The students were instructed to bring their completed notes sheet to class (part of our formative assessment). We posted the online activities assignment on our class website, as well as emailed the parents the assignment sheet with links (see Figure 8.5).

In Class—After the Flip!

Students had two days to complete the asynchronous part of the lesson. Many students completed the work at home, while others chose to access the information at our school library during study hours outside of class time. When the time came for us to apply the information they learned, there were noticeable sparks in the classroom. Classroom dialogue was rich with small-group and whole-class meaningful details and higher-level thinking. We provided "You Are the Teacher" time that allowed students in small groups to share with their peers. Furthermore, the students jumped right into the lab work without needing any lecturing or reteaching. We noticed that during the lab work, the students came to class with a deeper background knowledge base. They applied academic vocabulary, and they were actively engaged in applying their knowledge through the work and conversations. The completed guided notes sheet supported the students who needed scaffolding to increase the retention of content.

As another form of formative assessment, at the conclusion of class I asked the students to share out loud or write on a sticky note to let us know how they felt about this flipped learning experience. The theme of responses included being thankful to have the time to complete the assignment at their own pace ("I liked that I could keep rewatching the video until I really understood the fact." "I like learning at my own pace. It is hard to pay attention in class most of the time." "I felt more relaxed learning at home because I could replay and reread to help me understand.").

Other students were motivated by the options provided. "It made me want to learn more because there were these choices to click different links." Most students appreciated the guided notes. "The guided notes made it easier for me to remember the information—it went right along with the video, so it was easy to follow and understand." One student summed up the success of this flipped lesson by stating: "I just wish we had more time to be the teacher in class—I like taking charge of my own learning." This comment resonated even further with me because it came from a student who was typically quiet in class and hesitant to participate.

Name:_____ Date:_____

Moon Phases Guided Notes

What causes the moon phases—and why is the cycle consistent?

1. The phases of the moon represent the illuminated portions of the _____ that we see from _____.

2. As the moon orbits the _____, the sun's _____ reflects on the _____ causing a different part of the _____ to glow.

3. The moon has _____ main phases. They are:
    1. _____
    2. _____
    3. _____
    4. _____

4. It takes about one _____ for the moon to change from one _____ to another.

5. In between the phases the moon is either a _____, which means it's less than half full. Or it is a _____, which means it is more than half full.

6. When the moon appears to be growing, we say it is _____.

7. When the moon appears to be getting smaller, it is _____.

8. Sum It Up! Use these completed notes to answer this question:

    What causes the moon's phases—and why is the cycle consistent?

    ---------Write your answer on the back of this paper---------

© 2016 Elizabeth Stein

FIGURE 8.4. Guided notes for the seventh-grade flipped science lesson on phases of the moon

Name: _____   7th grade
Science

Get Ready to Be Amazed!

1. Check out this 3-minute video clip to learn about the **phases of the moon**. First watch and listen. And then watch it a second time, and complete the guided notes sheet to show us what you know!

2. **Now watch this cool video** to see the moon's phases in action! It's a really cool moon animation clip. First watch it straight through—be sure to notice the "view from Earth." Then watch and pause it every once in a while and use these vocabulary words to describe the phases that you notice.

Vocabulary:
1. full moon
2. first quarter (waxing quarter) half lit from the right
3. third quarter (waning quarter) half lit from the left
4. waxing gibbous
5. waning gibbous
6. waxing crescent
7. waning crescent

Name at least three phases that you noticed.

Optional BONUS material:

1. **Quizlet Flashcards**—Great for studying!

2. Video: **Interesting facts about the moon** and **more interesting facts here!**

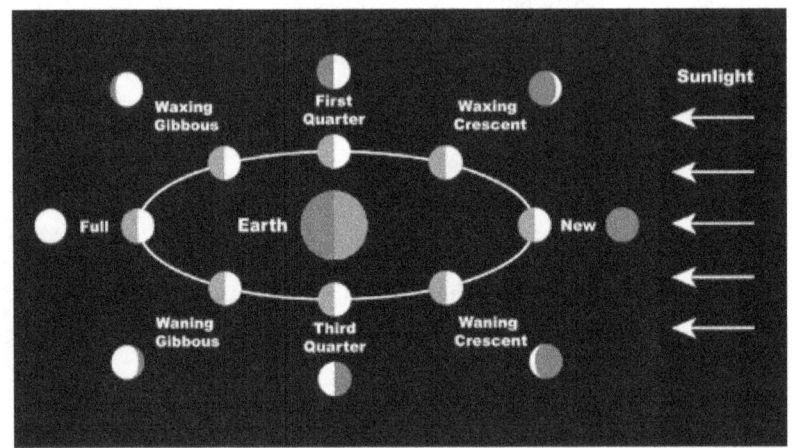

Image source: University of Delaware, https://ematusov.soe.udel.edu/science/moon-phases/index.htm

© 2016 Elizabeth Stein

FIGURE 8.5. Assignment sheet with links for the seventh-grade flipped learning science lesson

Now that you have an idea for outlining lesson plans without having to write a complete multipage plan, you see that you cover all necessary bases by writing down key elements that every lesson needs. It keeps you and your co-teacher strategic, focused, and flexible—not to mention you stay on top of applying a variety of relevant co-teaching models in the context of each lesson.

▶ Co-teaching Check-In

Colorful Conversation

Using a color wheel as a visual, take 30 seconds to view the image. Which color resonates with you in the moment? How does it connect with the way you are feeling about something that happened in class today? Each co-teacher should take turns sharing.

KEY TAKEAWAYS

✔ The Planning Prompt structure shares a time-saving yet comprehensive structure to co-plan.

✔ Flipped learning is a powerful way to engage in a co-teaching and learning process with all learners involved.

STUDY GROUP QUESTIONS

1. Share your current way of planning lessons. How do you involve your co-teacher?

2. How might the Planning Prompt approach elevate your co-planning and co-teaching process?

3. Describe your understanding of a flipped learning experience. What is one idea for your own future flipped lesson with your co-teacher and students?

9

More Strategies and Structures to Promote Learner Expertise

THE UDL GUIDELINES offer powerful and specific strategies to engage learners and help them become self-empowered, expert learners. Chapter 8 ignited our thinking around placing some UDL gears in motion when designing our lessons. This chapter extends our thinking by sharing more possibilities for co-teachers to elevate and expand their teaching and learning together with their students. These strategies will help you as co-teachers:

- Eliminate a sense of threat and create a comfortable, learner-centered environment.

- Facilitate complex, meaningful, real-world thinking.

- Respect the uniqueness of each learner.

- Provide peer support and specific feedback.

- Encourage self-monitoring and reflection as connected to learning goals.

- Promote active, relevant, choice-driven learning.

Expert learners know how to learn—not just in a particular class but everywhere they go.

As we know, our structural decisions are not enough. We must make sure that any co-teaching model and any teaching structure we apply is the frame for solid strategic and deep thinking through carefully designed instruction. Let's consider specific strategies that can illuminate any classroom with UDL. All strategies shared here may be effective for all grades and all content areas.

STRATEGIES FOR PROVIDING OPTIONS FOR STUDENT CHOICE

These strategies provide examples to keep students engaged, in control, and at the center of a meaningful learning process each day.

Choose Own Seats

This is a simple yet powerful way to empower learners. When teachers assign seats for students, that's saying to students, *I know what is best for you, and it doesn't matter if you think differently—I am the teacher and will make this decision.* Yet when students are given the options for seating, it can boost attention, behavior, and overall engagement. In the event that a student selects a seat that serves to distract the student and others from learning, you can use that as a teachable moment—or moments! Mention to the student that you notice they are distracted, and then ask them if they need your help to guide better choices.

> ### The UDL Connection
>
> **Engagement:** Students are empowered by the opportunity for choice, their ability to attend, and their ability to self-monitor their learning behaviors. These choices can minimize distractions and optimize motivation.
>
> **Action and Expression:** The process of peer collaboration and strategy development can be amplified through peer-to-peer interactions and flexible small groups during instructional time.
>
> **Co-teaching Tips:** Students can be allowed to sit anywhere they like, if the context of the lesson lends to this level of flexibility. Seating can be considered flexible as students move their desks and chairs according to the lesson and the day. There are two teachers, so the monitoring to ensure success is doubled. Clock Buddies (for elementary) or Assignment Buddies (for upper elementary and secondary) is also effective. Learn more at https://www.readingquest.org/clock_buddies.html.

Choice Boards

Choice boards are menus of activities that provide multiple options for students to explore and deepen their understanding on a given topic or concept. This strategy is effective in all content areas, including math, science, social studies, and English. When creating choice boards, teachers should consider the learning goal and key concepts for understanding. As choices are planned, make sure the key concepts and goals drive the activity options you develop. It is critical to connect the activity with the assessment of students' understanding and achievement toward the learning goal.

The UDL Connection

Engagement: The option to select activities increases motivation and optimizes autonomy. Students are easily focused on the goals and objectives by participating in meaningful activities. Students have the opportunity to take charge of their learning and work at their own pace.

Representation: Each activity may offer a variety of presentation modes. For example, one activity may link to a video and then ask students to reflect on the content. Another activity may offer the opportunity to analyze song lyrics or a graph or any visual that connects to the subject and concept.

Action and Expression: Each activity provides a different way to express one's understanding. For example, one activity may ask students to compose a song to describe a turning point in history or a section of a piece of literature. Another activity can ask students to write, act out, create a podcast, or design a poster or poem to express knowledge and understanding.

Co-teaching Tips: The power of two teachers to create activity options will highlight each other's area of expertise. One co-teacher may be savvy with technology, whereas the other is more artistic. The point is to combine the greatness each teacher has to offer. There is so much to learn from each other as well.

Choice of Assessment

When developing classroom assessments to determine a student's understanding of completed units of study, teachers typically give one test to all students. Why not offer them a test where you provide a few options for demonstrating their understanding? Allow students to choose between writing, speaking, and creating as a means of expressing any given concept. The key is to plan out your style of assessment over time to allow for an appropriate balance of developing the ability to gain knowledge and in responding to various types of assessment. For example, students should have practice with multiple-choice and essay questions, but that should not be the only style of assessment when considering learning through a UDL lens.

In addition, consider the voice of self-assessment as a tool for preparing students for an upcoming summative assessment. Prepare review sheets that guide students to code their level of understanding and prepare their focus for study.

The UDL Connection

Engagement: The opportunity for self-assessment creates a meaningful process for students reflect and connect with themselves as learners. Students gain a strong grasp on what they know and what they need to work on; they own their learning by persevering through challenges and celebrating their personal achievements.

Action and Expression: Students are given the opportunity to respond through varied methods of response.

Co-teaching Tips: Combine ideas for allowing the content and skills of your class to align with individual students' strengths and abilities. Meet the students where they are by coming together to plan your assessment procedures and formats. In addition, if the general education teacher plans an assessment, they should share it with the special education teacher, so that individual has plenty of time to review and add any UDL ideas—for example, perhaps a simple change in font size, formatting to include more space between questions, or more substantial changes that the teachers feel are appropriate. Both teachers should maintain the same high expectations for all learners.

Brainstorming Breaks

No matter what grade or subject you teach, make time for students to process. All learners need some time to take in the information that is presented. Allow time for students to reflect on segments of your lesson individually by jotting down their comments or questions in their notebooks. Another option is to strategically place chart paper around the room. Make time for a two- to four-minute pause for students to get out of their seats and write down their thoughts on the paper. The students may then take another two minutes to discuss their thinking in these small groups. These choices for brainstorming allow all students to participate compared to just brainstorming the whole class where only a few students share.

The UDL Connection

Engagement: All students have the opportunity to develop self-reflection skills rather than getting lost in the mix of a whole-class lesson where they too easily fall into the "let someone else participate" mode. This flexible brainstorming method fosters collaboration and increases the level of building a community of learners.

Representation: Students are exposed to the thinking of others through movement and written and oral expression. Students may also have the option to sketch their thoughts on the chart paper rather than write them down in words.

Action and Expression: The movement between listening, note-taking, and reflecting keeps learners alert and attentive. This reflective brainstorming and cooperative group learning strengthens learners' ability to monitor their understanding and increases their ability to communicate what they know and what they still wonder about.

Co-teaching Tips: The management piece is always an added bonus for strategies that require movement and monitoring. Since minimal to no preparation is involved, co-teachers can plan ahead or decide in the moments of teaching that this is a great way to keep learners engaged and learning.

Student Inquiry Teams

Setting up the structure for student inquiry teams takes a bit of planning, but it is a great way to provide choice and increase learning in any classroom. All you need to do is connect the subject area you teach with a few open-ended questions that would spark students' problem-solving and fact-finding skills.

It could be math equations or word problems, or it could be a question to support the themes and concepts in any content-area classroom. It is a great way to incorporate research skills as well.

The UDL Connection

Engagement: Providing a choice between questions for inquiry optimizes autonomy and motivation. The process of inquiry should wrap around clear goals for learning.

Representation: There are many ways teachers can introduce and support the process of these inquiry-based projects. Students may select from a list of teacher-generated questions. Teachers may provide students with links to take them to the class website or videos that spark the launch and process of this learning time.

Action and Expression: This peer-collaborative activity is deeply seated in choices. Students may be allowed to choose their teams. Or even if the teams are teacher selected, students have decisions to make as they direct their solution-seeking mindsets into action. Teachers can keep a stack of resources on tables around the room, so students can access these books and articles. Teachers can arrange for guest speakers to come and address some of the topics. And of course, technology through iPads, Chromebooks, or desktop computers provides boundless digital, multimedia resources. Check with your school librarian, who will be a wealth of information and ideas.

Co-teaching Tips: Students may gain further motivation by also creating their own questions to direct their learning. Consider providing the option for students to generate their ideas based on the concepts and topic of your class. An additional consideration may be to provide the choice for students to go solo. It is not always necessary to force collaboration when we are guiding learners. A healthy balance is key—especially for learners who have specific goals for working individually and in groups.

Hint Cards

This low-prep strategy guides metacognition and self-regulation. Hint cards encourage students to take control of their learning in real time. Oftentimes when students are asked to work independently, they struggle quietly or just sit unproductively until class time is over. Hint cards make supports available to all learners in the room. Students learn to self-regulate and ask deeper questions to guide their own learning.

Teachers decide on the challenging points in a learning activity where students may need additional support. It may be that students need a review of definitions or examples of previously taught concepts or vocabulary words. In math, hint cards can also include sample problems worked out step by step, so students can deepen their understanding of the mathematical thinking they need to apply to their work. The hint cards are placed strategically around the room.

The UDL Connection

Engagement: The threat of singling out struggling learners is minimized as the option is offered to all learners. As students choose to review the various hint cards, they may opt to discuss with peers to further their understanding. The movement around the room optimizes motivation as students select the level of support they need as the focus on learning goals stays strong.

Representation: Hint cards can be handwritten or typed printed cards. Teachers may also provide iPads or Chromebooks with a link for students to watch a video or view a website that may serve as a scaffold/hint to trigger deeper understanding and application.

Action and Expression: Hint cards can be prepared using multiple tools and technologies. Students build their fluency of knowledge at graduated levels of supports as they choose the hints they feel support their personal achievements.

Co-teaching Tips: This is a clear way to provide specific supports without singling any student out of the crowd. Students make the choice to use the hints as they see their peers use them and/or as they see the hints are offered to anyone who would like to use them. Co-teachers may need to coach the class and/or specific students with a gentle reminder that the hints are there and just waiting to be used. The Teaching Channel has a helpful video to see this strategy in action: https://www.teachingchannel.org/videos/hint-cards.

Flextime

There is something just so powerful about allowing students the freedom to use a specific amount of time in any way they choose, as long as it supports the learning that has been going on in class. Depending on the grade and subject, flextime is a great addition to class routines on a weekly or monthly basis. Students have the opportunity to empower their relationship with learning by selecting a specific task to practice or learn more about.

The UDL Connection

Engagement: This time is ideal for promoting personal strategic thinking. Learners decide how best to use this time as they expand their strategy applications and skills. Teachers may provide specific feedback to support students' mastery of specific goals.

Representation: Make a variety of tools and technologies available depending on your resources and on the specific tasks.

Action and Expression: Students work independently to build their knowledge and strategy base. This is an opportunity to optimize access to tools and technologies as appropriate for your resources and tasks for this time.

Co-teaching Tips: The flextime option optimizes any reteaching or explicit instruction that is needed for students with specific IEP goals. Both teachers should optimize this time to connect with students on their path to becoming expert learners. This is a perfect time for teachers to gain valuable formative assessment feedback on student performance.

SUPPORTING CONTENT-AREA READING, WRITING, LISTENING, AND SPEAKING

These strategies provide examples to guide learners to develop strategic thinking as they deepen their long-term connection with their learning process.

Scan, Question, Read, Write

The SQRW strategy (Strichart & Mangrum, 2002) naturally allows learners to follow the steps of effective reading by following four simple, manageable steps. Teachers can model and gradually release responsibility for students to be able to scan the text by noticing the text features, such as images, captions, titles, subtitles, and bold print. This step allows students to get ready to comprehend by previewing key features and connecting to what they already know.

- **Question:** Using each subtitle, the student selects one question word—*who, what, where, when, why, how*—and changes the subtitle into a question. The student structures their notepaper in a Q&A fashion.

- **Read:** Once the question is written down, the student is ready to read that section of the text with intention and purpose.

- **Write:** As the student identifies the response to the question, they write it down and get ready to write the question for the next section of reading.

The UDL Connection

Engagement: This strategy heightens the salience of the goals by having the student set a purpose and direct their reading comprehension throughout the reading time.

Representation: This strategy enhances textbook reading. It is also ideal for reading digital texts.

Action and Expression: Students have the option to write their notes in their notebooks, type their notes using technology, or work with a peer and take turns, with one peer being the speaker and the other writing down the notes.

Reciprocal Teaching

Reciprocal teaching (Palincsar & Brown, 1984) can transform any reading activity by guiding students to apply four active reading strategies: making predictions, asking questions, clarifying confusing words or phrases, and summarizing sections of the text. This strategy works well with literature and expository text and can be used in any grade. The teacher models reading a text by first making a prediction, and then continuing to model their thinking as they question, clarify, and summarize at various points in the text to demonstrate the natural flow and thinking during effective reading comprehension. The teacher moves to gradually release responsibility to the students as they practice with a peer. Students may take turns leading the group by facilitating the discussion at various points of the reading. These group leaders determine the section of reading that the students will complete. For example, the leaders say, "Okay, everyone read to the bottom of page X." The leader continues to lead the group with questions at strategic points of the reading, asking, "Who has a prediction? What questions do you have so far? Are there any confusing words or parts in the reading? Who wants to summarize what we read so far?" Students take turns being the leader (or teacher).

The UDL Connection

Engagement: This strategy encourages students to develop self-assessment of their reading and comprehension skills. In addition, they practice pushing through challenges as they realize that all readers get confused at points and that clarifying is part of the reading process for all readers. In addition, the group work fosters collaboration and community.

Representation: The text that students read can be presented in books, articles, or digital form. In addition, text-to-speech programs can be used if appropriate. Strategy cards can be labeled Predict, Clarify, Question, and Summarize to serve as a visual and manipulative tool for students to stay focused on the strategies. The strategies can also be presented on the SMART Board or as PowerPoint slides, anchor charts, or individual student bookmarks.

Action and Expression: Strategy development and goal-setting are supported through the natural reciprocal-teaching reading process. Students' ability to self-monitor their comprehension is naturally embedded. In addition, multiple tools for students to respond can be incorporated through oral expression, written expression, and use of technology.

Collaborative Strategic Reading

CSR (Klingner & Vaughn, 1999) is an effective strategy when guiding students to read content-area materials. The reading process involves four steps:

1. **Preview:** Students glance over text features to get an idea of what they are going to read as they connect to what they already know.

2. **Click and clunk:** Students work together to share what words and ideas they understood as key ideas (click) and what ideas or words they found confusing (clunk).

3. **Get the gist:** Students collaborate to summarize key points and paraphrase main ideas. In addition, they share why these ideas are important (the gist).

4. **Wrap-up:** After finishing the reading of all segments of the text, students summarize what they learned.

The UDL Connection

Engagement: Collaboration and community are fostered through group discussions.

Representation: Text may be in the form of textbooks, articles, or digital format. Cue cards for the four steps should be presented as a visual scaffold.

Action and Expression: Students focus on strategic thinking and self-monitoring. In addition, they build fluency and stamina to deepen their ability to read more complex texts. Multimedia such as speech-to-text or text-to-speech options can be incorporated.

Co-teaching Tips: Consider the strengths of your students and assign a role to specific individuals to guide other students to take a leadership role in this reading-group process. Make sure to scaffold the reading and writing process to knock down any barriers that prevent students from accessing and participating in this learning experience.

Interactive Notebooks

This strategy teaches students to take any class lesson, concept, or lecture and transform the key points into meaningful notes and learning opportunities. Each student has a notebook dedicated to a specific subject area (math, science, social studies, English, study skills). Students use the right side of the notebook to glue the class notes from any particular day. The left side is for students to respond to those class notes. The idea is to give students time to process important information or concept(s). Student may choose to paraphrase, sketch, transfer information to a graphic organizer, or use some other way to deepen their understanding so that they connect and transfer the information.

The UDL Connection

Engagement: Students make the choice for how they will express their understanding on the left side of the page. They reflect and self-assess to gain deeper understanding.

Representation: Although the class notes that go on the right side of the page will be in the form of text or graphics, the instruction that surrounds the notes may include multimedia representations.

Action and Expression: Students have the option to sketch, write, and engage in discussions as they decide how to express their understanding on the left side of the notebook.

Co-teaching Tips: It is easy to individualize the process of creating these notebooks. Be sure to encourage each learner to apply their area of strength and talent to creating their understanding. Include peer interactions to spark each learner to connect to their understanding. Peer interactions can be a powerful process for connecting the learning with the learner.

Question–Answer–Detail

The QAD strategy encourages students to organize the process of sifting through key ideas when reading, listening, and/or creating meaningful notes to remember important information. This three-column notes organizer guides students through a sequential thinking process as they expand their understanding on a given topic or concept. The questions may be teacher generated to guide students' focus and inquiry, or teachers may decide to ask students to create the questions to provide the opportunity for higher-level thinking. Questions should be generated based on what teachers want students to know about a particular topic. Questions are the driving force as they direct students to listening or reading to locate the answer and gather details to extend their knowledge.

The UDL Connection

Engagement: QAD promotes expectations and focused strategy use to guide attention and motivation.

Representation: Students are guided to process information by visualizing the QAD sequence to organize their thinking.

Action and Expression: Multimedia options can be used to generate the notes. As students respond to questions, they increase their ability to self-monitor their performance by finding text evidence to verify their responses.

Co-teaching Tips: You may scaffold the process by allowing students to work in pair or in groups. You can include digital options such as typing or engaging with speech-to-text technologies.

Fact, Question, Response

FQR (Harvey & Goudvis, 2007) is a three-column note-taking strategy that provides a visual structure to guide students' comprehension and deeper understanding about the content. In the column labeled "Facts," students list a few important facts about the topic or concept that they are responsible for knowing. This could be in preparation for reading a text, listening to a lecture, or viewing a video. Next to each fact, in the "Question" column, students write down a question that comes to mind during the learning experience. Following the learning, students write a response to their question as it connects to the listed fact. The response should deepen their understanding of the fact by guiding students to pose a question and seek a meaningful response.

The UDL Connection

Engagement: Learners set a purpose for their reading, listening, or viewing by formulating a question based on the selected fact.

Representation: Texts and/or technology can easily be incorporated to present the content. Access to the internet can be an added way to present information through videos, podcasts, online images, and so forth.

Action and Expression: Teachers can design the process and products to allow students to write, speak, and sketch as they create facts, questions, and responses. In addition, cooperative groups can be formed to allow peers to assign roles to one another for speaking, researching, writing, and so forth.

Co-teaching Tips: If students are reading a text, you can provide them with three different-colored sticky notes—for example, "Facts" written on blue stickies, "Questions" written on yellow stickies, and "Responses" written on green stickies. Students may place their stickies on a small-group or whole-class chart to allow them to learn from one another. In addition, teachers may want to begin with teacher-selected facts to guide a focus on specific knowledge their students need to know.

Connect, Collect, Correct

Connect, Collect, Correct (Carreker, 2004) is a powerful three-column note-taking organizer that promotes strategic thinking and world knowledge by tapping into students' background knowledge prior to a reading, listening, or viewing exercise. Students jot down what they know about the topic or concept and then, as they read, listen, or view the content, they record details about the topic. Students check for understanding during the moments of learning and add their new thinking in the "Correct" column. I like to add "Confirm" to the "Collect" column when students' background knowledge and collection of details align with their new, expanded views. Students learn to integrate new information.

The UDL Connection

Engagement: This strategy promotes active reading, listening, and speaking. In addition, teachers may incorporate peer/class discussions to incorporate collaboration.

Representation: Teachers have the flexibility to apply digital presentations, text presentations, and use of audio modes for presenting information.

Action and Expression: Use of multiple means of media and communication are evident through thoughtful instructional design. Teachers have the flexibility to design learning around multiple tools for constructing knowledge.

Co-teaching Tips: Consider opening the lesson with a quick review through engaging video or other visuals along with class discussion to trigger background knowledge for students before having them write their initial connections.

Card Pyramid

A card pyramid (Carreker, 2004) may be used to organize main ideas and supporting details and facts through this visual scaffold to guide their oral or written summaries. This strategy has a lot of flexibility in the way teachers want to apply it. You can use index cards so students can move the cards around as a visual-kinesthetic reminder to keep them on track. You can also use colored felt squares that you prepare for students to use. For example, you may cut a blue square to symbolize the main idea, and yellow squares to indicate each detail that supports that main idea. Figure 9.1 shows another version where I covered cardboard blocks to create a block pyramid with paper and labeled it with "Main idea" and "Supporting detail" to guide fourth- and fifth-grade students to include three details to support the main idea of a text. This visual and kinesthetic scaffold guided the students' thinking. This block pyramid works well to include the visual and kinesthetic as well as the added auditory excitement of the blocks falling if the students' summary or explanation needed more organization and details. If the students did not include a strong main idea to support the details, the pyramid fell down and crashed, which caused them to smile and push through the challenge to build their thinking more clearly.

FIGURE 9.1. Block pyramid

The UDL Connection

Engagement: Students are focused on the goal of zooming in on main ideas and key details. Students have the opportunity for increased attention and motivation as a result of the visual and kinesthetic scaffolding.

Representation: Teachers have the option to present information in ways where they maximize the use of available resources. The teachers' creative side has room to grow here.

Action and Expression: Options for multiple means of communication and knowledge-building are left to the teachers' connection between resources and specific needs of students in class. Teachers have the opportunity to allow students to process and express ideas in ways that connect with their individual strengths.

- **Co-teaching Tips:** Connect students' individual IEP goals with this activity to ensure heightened success with expressing main ideas and details. Consider peer interactions to support collaborative options. The block pyramid is another version of the card pyramid strategy to guide students' oral and/or written expression to include clear, concise main ideas and details following reading or listening to a text or lesson.

Concept Circles

Concept circles (Vacca et al., 2021) are a quick, easy-to-implement visual for remembering key vocabulary words that expand students' understanding of important concepts and themes. Each concept circle has a heading to indicate the concept, and then students add the vocabulary words to demonstrate deeper understanding as they expand their vocabulary. See Figure 9.2 for a sample concept circle around the Westward Expansion. Students may add sketches and words next to, or on the back of, the concept circle to add details to this great visual and study guide.

The UDL Connection

Engagement: Vary the demands and resources for students as they complete the concept circles to optimize attention and motivation.

Representation: A variety of texts, videos, website links, podcasts, and so forth may be set up for students to explore and build their background knowledge and review of the concept.

Action and Expression: An additional way to apply concept circles is by having students fill in the concept circles based on their class notes and background knowledge base only. This introduces the additional process of self-monitoring what they know in preparation for a summative or formative assessment. They may then evaluate what they know and expand their knowledge by seeking available multimedia resources.

Co-teaching Tips: Be sure to provide explicit small-group instruction to instill the importance and process of selecting keywords. Oftentimes, students have difficulty determining what is most important to remember. Guide the process and release the responsibility to them as they are ready, then observe and listen to what they do and say!

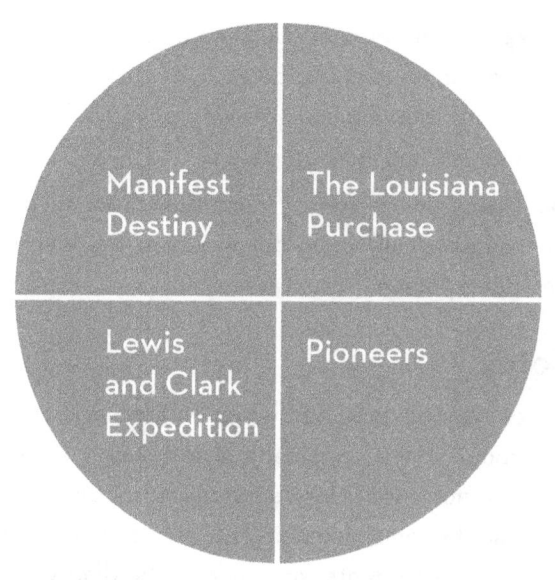

FIGURE 9.2. Concept circle for the Westward Expansion

Exclusion Brainstorming

Exclusion brainstorming (Blachowicz 1986) is an effective way to create student-led discussions and critical thinking skills. The teacher presents a word cloud or list of words related to a given topic or concept. Students work as a team, small groups, or as a whole class to decide what words should be eliminated because they do not capture the essence of the main topic. This strategic process encourages students to evaluate the facts and their understanding. Students must justify their thinking as they decide to keep or eliminate listed words. This process guides learners to determine importance while learning.

The UDL Connection

Engagement: Strategic thinking is encouraged as students are given the choice to decide what words to eliminate, and then asked to justify and explain their thinking.

Representation: Digital tools such as EdWordle (http://www.edwordle.net/), teacher-created PowerPoint or SMART Board slides, and so forth can be used. In addition, good old-fashioned markers and chart paper can be a good way to go.

Action and Expression: Students become engaged in a process of collaboration by calling out answers and deleting or crossing words off the list on the board. Students' listening and speaking skills are highlighted to extend strategy development and communication.

Co-teaching Tips: Consider giving students individual copies of the words so that they may physically cross out words as the learning unfolds, thus providing an added personal visual as well.

Blackout Notes

During content-area reading, provide the option for blackout notes. Take a few minutes to read through the reading material and cross out any words, phrases, or sentences that are not critical for comprehension. Once these are blacked out, the students read the remaining text. This makes the reading more manageable and direct for those students who need scaffolding with comprehension and remembering the most important facts from content-area reading. Figure 9.3 shows an example of this strategy in practice.

The UDL Connection

Engagement: This strategy may optimize value in reading as students see that they have to read only the most essential parts of the text. It may also minimize the perceived threat of needing to read extensive notes to make reading more manageable. Students may also be more motivated to read since they are guided to read the most essential information only.

Representation: The process of reading with the blackout notes strategy promotes understanding vocabulary by simplifying the structure of the reading passage. This strategy may guide students to process the most important concepts and vocabulary, and as a result, to internalize and generalize the information with greater success.

Action and Expression: This strategy guides students to become more fluent in expressing their understanding of the content through graduated levels of support. As the students build their stamina for reading, fewer words may be blacked out.

Co-teaching Tips: Co-teachers are encouraged to provide blackout notes to the students and, over time, work with students as partners to black out the notes together. This process will guide students to determine importance in text as well as help teachers monitor their comprehension.

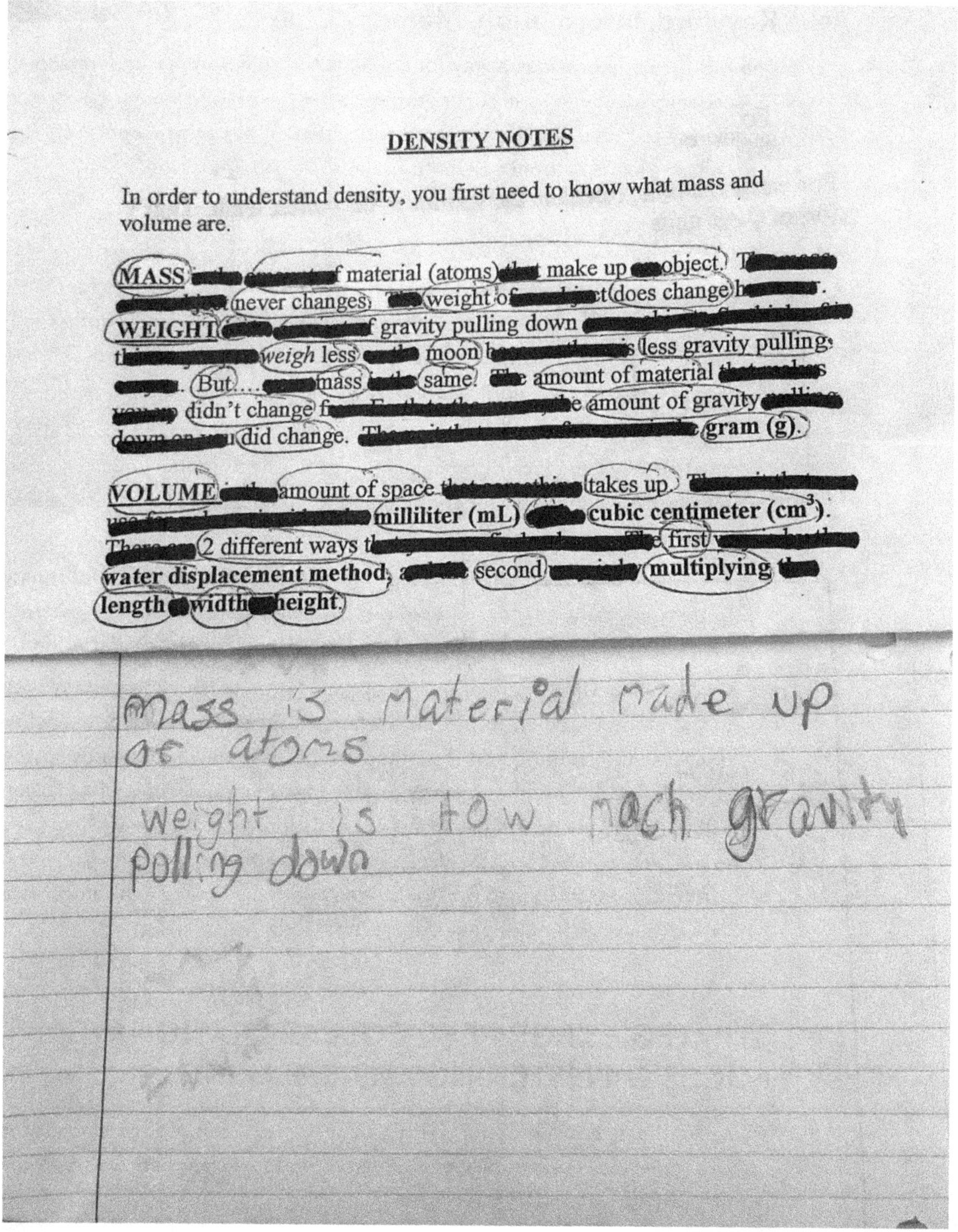

DENSITY NOTES

In order to understand density, you first need to know what mass and volume are.

MASS ~~is the amount of~~ material (atoms) ~~that~~ make up ~~an~~ object. ~~The mass of an object~~ never changes, ~~but the~~ weight ~~of an object~~ does change ~~because~~...
WEIGHT ~~is the amount of~~ gravity pulling down ~~on an object~~... ~~things~~ weigh less ~~on the~~ moon ~~because there is~~ less gravity pulling... But... ~~the~~ mass ~~is the~~ same. The amount of material ~~that makes~~ ~~you~~ didn't change ~~from Earth to the moon, the~~ amount of gravity ~~pulling~~ down ~~on you~~ did change. ~~The unit that~~... gram (g).

VOLUME ~~is the~~ amount of space ~~that something~~ takes up. ~~The units that are used for volume are~~ milliliter (mL) ~~and~~ cubic centimeter (cm³). ~~There are~~ 2 different ways ~~to find volume~~. The first ~~is the~~ water displacement method, ~~and the~~ second ~~is by~~ multiplying ~~the~~ length × width × height.

---

mass is material made up of atoms

weight is how much gravity pulling down

FIGURE 9.3. Blackout notes

Keyword, Information, Memory Clue

The KIM strategy provides a way for students to organize their understanding for academic vocabulary and concepts by using keywords and learner-generated mnemonics to guide working memory and retention of key concepts. See Figure 9.4 for an example from a seventh-grade social studies lesson.

The UDL Connection

Engagement: The process of this strategy increases opportunities for teachers to provide mastery-oriented feedback based on students' work. Motivation is also optimized as students engage in the creative process while teachers actively monitor their understanding of the content.

Representation: The tri-column notes provide a visual organizational structure that may further clarify vocabulary. The finished product becomes a personalized representation for comprehending and generalizing understanding of key concepts and vocabulary.

Action and Expression: This strategy provides students with the opportunity to think critically, flexibly, and creatively as they paraphrase and illustrate their understanding of key vocabulary through quick sketches and writing.

Co-teaching Tips: There are many options for co-teachers to engage with this strategy together. It may be a whole-class lesson where one teacher discusses the content, and the other teacher is modeling notes using the strategy. In addition, the strategy may be used during a whole-class lesson with the teachers pausing at strategic points for students to work in groups to complete their KIM notes. Also, consider using this strategy with a focus on small-group instruction to provide students with the time to think and create individually and through peer discussions.

STRATEGIES FOR PEER COLLABORATION WITH FOCUS ON LISTENING AND SPEAKING

These strategies provide opportunities for fostering a sense of community, as the UDL principles are naturally embedded to bridge a clear path between the content and each learner in the classroom.

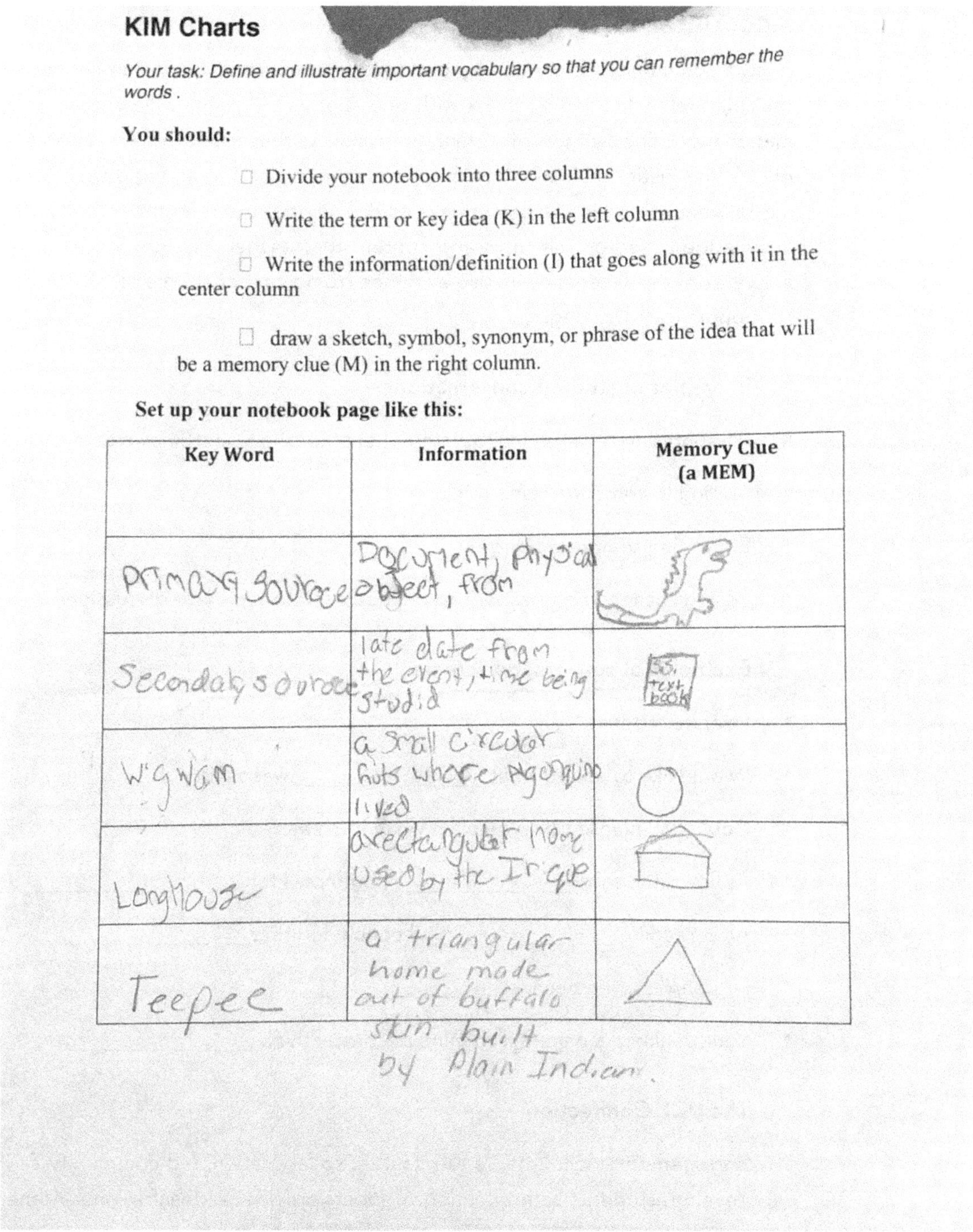

KIM Charts

Your task: Define and illustrate important vocabulary so that you can remember the words.

You should:

- [ ] Divide your notebook into three columns
- [ ] Write the term or key idea (K) in the left column
- [ ] Write the information/definition (I) that goes along with it in the center column
- [ ] draw a sketch, symbol, synonym, or phrase of the idea that will be a memory clue (M) in the right column.

Set up your notebook page like this:

Key Word	Information	Memory Clue (a MEM)
Primary source	Document, physical object, from	*(sketch of dinosaur)*
Secondary source	late date from the event, time being studied	SS textbook
Wigwam	a small circular huts where Algonquin lived	○
Longhouse	a rectangular home used by the Iroquoise	*(house sketch)*
Teepee	a triangular home made out of buffalo skin built by Plain Indian.	△

FIGURE 9.4. KIM vocabulary

Accountable Talk

Build a community of learners by providing students with opportunities to use their natural inclination to speak with one another. Students will process information more deeply through active discussion as they listen to the thoughts of others and justify their own thinking. Students respond to and add their thinking to what others in the group have said. They discuss relevant and accurate knowledge based on the topic and content the teachers design. Students are active, attentive listeners who use evidence from a text or source of information to support their thinking.

Examples of student conversations

- Paraphrasing or repeating to clarify what others have said (known as *revoicing*)
- Adding to someone else's thinking
- Explaining their reasoning
- Posing challenging questions to dig deeper into topics for discussion

Examples of conversation stems

- I wonder about . . .
- I would like to add to what _____ was saying.
- Could you please clarify/explain what you mean?
- At first, I thought _____, but now I think _____.
- After reading _____, I concluded that _____.
- I agree/disagree because _____.
- Your thinking connects with mine because I think _____.

The UDL Connection

Engagement: Accountable talk fosters collaboration and community as it develops students' self-reflection. Students provide feedback to one another as they share their thinking. Teachers also contribute to deepen the richness of discussions as needed.

Representation: Student conversations as well as the conversation stems make a perfect anchor chart for the classroom. In addition, you may decide to make them a digital slide and present it as needed. You can give students topics or questions for discussion after they view a video, navigate a website and digital text, or read a book, article, or information listed on index cards.

Action and Expression: Listening and speaking are encouraged with this strategy, yet students may have additional methods as options for communication. For example, you can have one student take the minutes and type or write down the conversation to be used for future studying and discussion.

Co-teaching Tips: Remember the value of UDL and additional scaffolds through SDI; make sure that each group has the right amount of challenge along with supports to master communication skills as they gain meaningful knowledge on the topic of discussion. Each group, and each student in each group, does not have to be doing the same thing.

Lansdown Word Cards

Sharon Lansdown (1991) designed this strategy as a way to actively involve her students in remembering key ideas and vocabulary during a lesson. Here's one way to apply the strategy:

1. Teacher(s) determine the topic of the lesson and prepare index cards, with one key vocabulary word per card.

2. Each student receives a card and is asked to hold up their card as the word is spoken during the lesson.

3. As the students hold up their cards, the teacher may decide to pause to discuss the term in the context of the lesson and overall concept.

Students learn vocabulary in context as well as gain active listening skills and increased background knowledge.

The UDL Connection

Engagement: This strategy fosters a sense of community as students look around to see who is holding up word cards and then participating in class discussions.

Representation: Word cards may be presented with graphics and images to extend the students' understanding.

Action and Expression: Listening and speaking are highly encouraged to strengthen students' communication skills. The use of technology to extend class discussions can deepen the experience as students learn new ideas and concepts. Students may spend time in peer collaborations matching definition of words with the context sentences to illustrate the meaning of words for greater retention. Words are selected from content-area subjects and/or literature.

Co-teaching Tips: Peer tutoring can be used to increase motivation and student understanding. As words are raised, allow time for students to discuss the meaning of each word within the context of the lesson. You may differentiate the complexity of the words given to students by strategically handing out the word cards.

Text on Text

Groups of three to five students gather around one large-print copy of a text. Each student uses a different color marker to write comments, connections, or questions based on their reading of the text. Students may respond to one another's comments as well. Then, the whole class joins in a gallery walk (see the gallery walk strategy later in this chapter) to read and write comments generated by other groups. Oral discussions may also occur in groups or as a whole class. See Figures 9.5 and 9.6.

The UDL Connection

Engagement: This strategy fosters a strong sense of collaboration and community as students share and learn about one another's perspectives. Options for self-regulation are naturally embedded as students decide what to share through their collaborations. They also extend their thinking by adding on to peers' comments, which optimizes motivation.

Representation: You can spur creativity by presenting texts on poster paper with colorful markers. You can also present text on Chromebooks or iPads, and students can use speech-to-text technology to document their thinking.

FIGURE 9.5. Student active reading sample

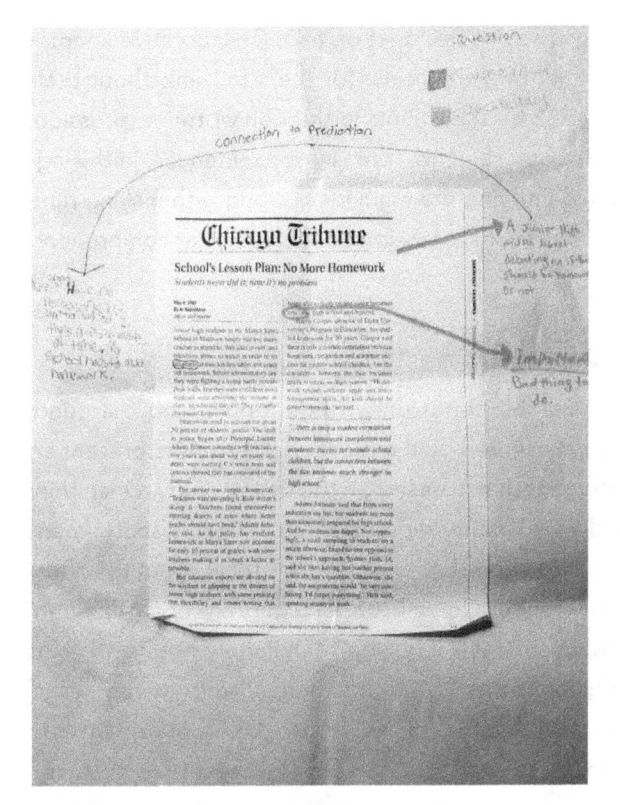

FIGURE 9.6. Collaborative annotations

Action and Expression: The process of this collaboration is typically through written discussions until later on when all comments have been added. Teachers may decide to include oral expression throughout the process if it is in the best interest of students' needs. In addition, students can be encouraged to sketch their ideas, so invite them to draw.

Co-teaching Tips: It is a good idea to model the process of this strategy. Co-teachers may demonstrate how it is done, and then hang up their finished product as a model and visual scaffold for students. In Figure 9.5, these seventh-grade students decided to provide a key for active reading to guide their thinking (see the upper-right corner). They provided their own additional scaffold, which is evidence of effective self-monitoring and reflection. Talk about engagement!

In Figure 9.6, students engage in written text on text. Collaborative annotations deepen readers' thinking by providing time for them to think about their understanding of the topic, then share their thinking through written expression. Students are free to jot down words, sketches, phrases, or sentences. In this figure, these students reflect on identifying the main idea—along with making time to express how collaborative annotations are helping them to better comprehend the text.

Corners: Get Up and Go!

With this strategy, students have the opportunity to get up and move around, and ponder the topic/concept presented by the teacher(s). Teachers present an open-ended question or statement that is based on the unit of study. Once they settle on the question, they decide on the degrees of agreement/disagreement and post each on a card around the room. For example, let's think about the question "Should we celebrate Christopher Columbus?" The degrees of agreement/disagreement could be "Yes, absolutely!" "Maybe," "Definitely not!" and "Not sure yet . . . I am still thinking about that." Students then move to the corner of the room that states how they feel. As students move into their groups, teachers give students a few minutes to discuss what they feel—and why they feel that way. The activity ends as the whole class comes together to share the main discussions from each group. Teachers can also opt to have students write down their responses in addition to speaking with peers.

The UDL Connection

Engagement: Learning is stimulated through movement, which can keep learners more alert and motivated. Peer interactions foster a sense of collaboration as learners gain a stronger sense of autonomy and personal opinions based on facts.

Representation: Providing students this time to think more deeply about a topic or concept maximizes transfer and deeper understandings. Visual scaffolds such as videos, graphics, illustrations, and texts can be offered to guide information processing and synthesizing.

Action and Expression: Students' listening, oral communication, critical thinking, and decision-making are highlighted. The integration of movement to a specific section of the room provides a voice for those students who may not be ready to speak out loud. Students can also be given the option to record their discussions and play back for the whole class to listen and discuss further.

Co-teaching Tips: Clarify and review any vocabulary with visual scaffolds or a quick review before you have the students move to their group.

Points to Ponder

Let's face it: There are times when students just need to listen to a lecture, a video, a conversation, or any chunks of information. It is important for teachers to remember to stop and pause at strategic points to allow students to process and attach meaning to the information. At these stop points the teacher(s) should model the "points to ponder." What are those key points that need further thinking and clarification? Share out loud and create a list of these points to guide students' thinking.

The UDL Connection

Engagement: Information is provided within a reasonable amount of time to maximize processing and retention, which easily facilitates coping and strategy skill development. Students' sense of community will come into play in this relaxed, stimulating learning environment.

Representation: Information can be represented in ways that suit the subject and specific style of the teacher, students, and resources available.

As the information is presented (with the idea that multimedia maximizes presenting information in ways to meet all learners in the context of the lesson), students have time to clarify vocabulary and concepts during the stop points as the teacher guides deeper awareness to ponder and think more deeply.

Action and Expression: Students deepen their understanding by listening to the teachers' think-aloud. Students can work in pairs, small groups, or solo as they decide what points are important to ponder at that point of the lesson. In addition, this "points to ponder" time provides students with the opportunities to self-monitor their progress and understanding. You may even decide to have students jot down their points as added written expression or sketch their ideas to document their thinking.

Co-teaching Tips: You can plan ahead for some or all of the stop points, but be flexible in the moment as you notice how your students are responding and adjust stop points as needed.

Peer-to-Peer Think-Aloud

Sometimes students need time to think about the information without teachers getting in the way! Here's a way to break up lectures or longer segments of any lesson. Stop every so often to allow your students to process how they connect the lesson with their background knowledge. Allow students to do one of two ideas (their choice!):

1. Repeat an important fact or idea that you just heard and share how it connects to something you already know.

2. Pose a question: What is confusing you at this point in the lesson?

Give students a few minutes to share with one another. If questions arise and students still need clarifications, either make time to respond right then and there or collect students' questions and be sure to catch up with the students after class.

The UDL Connection

Engagement: This strategy guides students to develop a sense of reflection. They begin to value and trust their instincts. They become eager to ask questions and to advocate for themselves as learners when they are given the time and space to exercise this right.

Representation: Always think in terms of providing options for auditory and visual information. Seek out available resources that will match the context of each specific lesson.

Action and Expression: Providing this time for students to collaborate and process and synthesize the content with their own thinking allows for graduated levels of support and practice as students are given this time to think—really think.

Co-teaching Tips: Co-teachers should monitor the discussions with the pairs of students but should not interject or get involved unless they see students need guidance to get on a clear-thinking path. Peer-to-peer think-aloud and interaction time can be valuable learning and leading time as students build confidence to process and share their thinking.

Paraphrasing Ticket

Any content-area subject requires students to remember and communicate key academic vocabulary words to demonstrate their knowledge. Making time for students to express what they learned in their own words is one of the most empowering strategies. Students become confident in expressing their ideas, the facts, their questions, and their beliefs when they are given additional practice to articulate their thoughts out loud and in writing. Make time for students to complete a "paraphrase ticket" at the end of a lesson, at the end of class, or any time you feel it is appropriate to guide their academic communications.

The UDL Connection

Engagement: Making the time to paraphrase key understandings highlights the goals and objectives of any lesson. In addition, students begin to develop deeper reflections and self-assessment within the process of any lesson because they become comfortable with putting facts and concepts into their own words.

Representation: Think multimedia. Think about your available resources. Think about how you can present your lesson in a way that supports students' background knowledge and processing of important information.

Action and Expression: This is a great way to increase students' written expression because these are short, quick writes where students gain practice within a relaxed environment.

Co-teaching Tips: Vary the methods of response as needed. Students may sketch, verbalize, or act out any concepts as they paraphrase key points.

Gallery Walk

A gallery walk is a great way to get students up and moving as they gain knowledge and communication skills in any class or lesson. Teacher(s) share an open-ended question or statement with students. Students work in groups to respond to this question by creating a group poster. Once each group has completed their poster, they hang it up or place it on a table around the room. The class then circulates around the room so each group may explore and learn from one another.

A spokesperson from each group may stay by their group's work to answer any questions or provide further details.

The UDL Connection

Engagement: Peer collaborations deepen a sense of community in the classroom. During the creation of the posters, students have a clear focus on the goals of the lesson, and they have the freedom of choice as they decide how to create their response.

Representation: The lesson that leads up to the gallery walk may be presented in a way that makes sense with meeting the needs of the learning objectives and the students. Academic vocabulary can be supported through anchor charts and the use of individual thesaurus books or apps on an iPad or Chromebook for students to clarify any vocabulary needed to create their poster.

Action and Expression: Students can use any media that the teacher(s) have available. Art supplies can be brought in for students to draw, paint, and illustrate their ideas. Chromebooks or iPads can be used for students to create a blog post, podcast, or PowerPoint or Prezi slide.

Co-teaching Tips: Monitor the flow of the movement and conversations to ensure maximum learning. You may opt to have students leave comments on a sticky note or on a sheet of paper to provide feedback to each group. Teachers, don't forget to leave your specific feedback to each group as well.

Learning Links

In small groups, students jot down their ideas to support an open-ended question or the task of summarizing the key points of any given topic or subject. Each student jots down their idea and places it in the center of the table. The students spend time reading each other's ideas and decide how each response connects to the lesson or unit of study. Students create one thematic sentence to illustrate a central idea to their thinking.

The UDL Connection

Engagement: Students value their thinking and the thinking of their peers through meaningful discussions.

Representation: Students identify and build upon their background knowledge. Information processing is guided through shared written and oral expressions. Multimedia options may easily be incorporated to illustrate ideas in a variety of ways.

Action and Expression: Students can write on sticky notes, chart paper, sentence strips, or dry-erase boards. Digital tools such as Padlet (www.padlet.com) can be used to allow students to jot their ideas down on a digital forum.

Co-teaching Tips: If you would like to focus on oral expression and an easily flowing conversation, then each group can select one "reporter" to write down student comments. Additionally, students can sketch their ideas and create captions to label their sketch for clarification purposes.

Line-Ups

The line-ups approach is a structured way to get students out of their seats and thinking on their feet. Simply arrange students in two lines. Organize the lines in whatever way suits the physical space in your room (either next to each other or one line at the left side of the room and the other line at the right). One teacher stands at the front of the board and asks a question based on a recently taught subject matter. The teacher stands back and allows the students at the head of each line to take turns responding to the question. It may be posed in competition style if that serves to motivate and stimulate the learning, or each student from each line may collaborate to respond.

Once that question and its answer are discussed, the front students go to the end of the line, and the next question and next two students come up. Co-teachers take turns asking questions and monitoring students' attention. See Figure 9.7 for an example of how the line-up strategy was used in one fourth-grade class as the teachers provided additional time for the students to practice their multiplication facts.

The UDL Connection

Engagement: You can focus on collaboration and building knowledge and fluency of facts within a community of learners.

Representation: Material and content can be represented in a variety of formats. Teachers should select a method of representation that suits the specific lesson. For example, if this activity is implemented to review for an upcoming content-area assessment, teachers can prepare index cards to read with a variety of questions to target the information the students need to know. Another way to present the material is through digital PowerPoint slides with questions and answers visually scaffolded for the students.

Action and Expression: Getting students up and out of their seats is always a good idea to keep them alert and as focused as possible. Students strengthen their oral and/or written expression communication skills as they participate in the planned activity.

Co-teaching Tips: Anchor charts can be used as visual scaffolds to trigger memory of key terms to scaffold accuracy and fluency. In addition, teachers should consider reminding students that they need to give one another "time to think" to allow wait time for students to process and respond with their best efforts and abilities.

FIGURE 9.7. Example of how the line-up approach was used in one fourth-grade classroom to practice multiplication facts

✔ **Co-teaching Check-In Activity**

How About We Try This?!

Each co-teacher selects one new strategy they would like to try within the next month. Plan to implement one strategy at least three different times over the next month. After the strategy is applied three times, discuss how it went. What were the benefits for specific students and the class as a whole? How could you continue to use the strategy? How could you adapt the strategy to create better access for meaningful learning with specific students and with class as a whole?

KEY TAKEAWAYS

✔ All classrooms—any subject, any grade—may elevate instruction by designing with UDL in mind.

✔ The UDL Guidelines provide a clear structure for teachers to apply specific strategies and structures to meet the needs of variable learners in the room.

✔ Strategies are the instructional decisions that guide deeper thinking within the structure of classroom routines, co-teaching models, and UDL principles and guidelines.

STUDY GROUP QUESTIONS

1. Explain what I mean by *creative structure*. How does it make room for students to take charge of their own learning? What is one upcoming lesson you may structure creatively?

2. Explain how the co-teaching models support effective instruction within inclusive, co-teaching settings.

3. Extending your thinking from your response to question 1, explain why co-teaching models are not enough. How can the UDL principles and guidelines serve as a strong framework for elevating instruction within each co-taught lesson?

4. Let's apply a 3-2-1 strategy to this question:
   - Name three strategies from this chapter that you would like to apply in your classroom.
   - Share two connections you made as you read through this chapter on structures and strategies.
   - Name one strategy from this chapter or from your own repertoire of strategies and explain how it can support the variable learners in your classroom. Use the UDL Guidelines as a reference to support your thinking.

PART 3

In the School: Partnering With Administrators, Community, and Caregivers

10

Elevating Partnerships With Administrators

LET'S GET RIGHT to the point: When administrators are part of co-teaching teams, there is increased opportunity for elevating co-teaching. In my experiences, the administrative presence must be consistent to allow for a meaningful and evolving partnership. Since writing the first edition, I have fine-tuned and created strategies that provide opportunities to forge strong partnerships that balance the evaluative administrative role with organic, humanizing practices.

This chapter will review two examples of successful (and realistic!) partnerships with administrators that I share as a result of my own co-teaching experiences (over the past 30 years) as well as my experiences working with administrative teams across the nation since writing the first edition of this book. Each example describes how administrators may visibly support co-teachers within the busy schedules of daily routines.

TWO EXAMPLES OF ADMINISTRATORS AS PARTNERS IN THE CLASSROOM

The first example is the "Let's Do This!" partnership, which embodies co-creating a culture of collaboration in the building or district. The second example is the "Sounds Great!" partnership, which supports an individual classroom phenomenon. Let's take a closer look at each partnership.

"Let's Do This!" Direct Team Approach

Some effective co-teaching partnerships begin with administrative supports and initiatives. These ideal experiences reveal administrators who embrace the value of co-teaching, make it a priority to integrate professional development along with honoring consistent co-planning time within the master schedule, and offer other supports to optimize co-teaching practices. They have a presence in classrooms, the hallway, and the building as a whole. This presence may include some or all of the following: participating in lessons, co-planning time, and connecting with students in the moments of instruction. They also make time for private conversations with co-teachers as needed to address classroom-oriented topics and events. Relationships are created that foster meaningful communication and supports. Furthermore, these administrators create collaboration by listening to how the co-teachers are experiencing teaching and learning and continue to work with the aim to continually improve together. Faculty meetings incorporate co-teaching and teaching diverse learners as a natural part of each school day. The benefits of co-teaching and feeling a sense of inclusivity are present within the classrooms and the entire building.

"Sounds Great!" Indirect Team Approach

Another effective partnership between administrators and co-teachers is what I call the "Sounds Great!" experience. In this type, teachers feel comfortable going to the administrator for advice or to share ideas, questions, and updates. The administrator may not initiate the collaboration, but the teachers feel comfortable and supported. The administrator is there as needed and aware, yet not directly a part of what is happening in the classroom. Professional development focuses on other important topics. However, if the teachers reach out for approval in co-teaching professional development, the administrator will facilitate their attendance. What happens inside the walls of their classroom feels like co-teaching bliss in the making. Yet, the magic stays in their classroom.

HOW ADMINISTRATORS CAN SUPPORT CO-TEACHERS

The two examples of administrative partnerships reveal the need for administrators to actively support the co-teaching experience. The visible supports are strong enough to illuminate an intangible sense of empowerment that the co-teachers feel, which translates into their classroom applications. Although a building-wide cultural experience is the ideal we should all aim for, co-teaching may work well as long as support is present at the classroom level. The two strategies just described embody the spirit of elevating co-teaching through UDL because they focus on attending to what is working as a way to continue strengthening areas that need improvement. Team members can transform their practice as they become keenly aware of current ideas and situations while remaining open to improving—together, through valuing multiple perspectives.

Here are additional ways administrators can support effective co-teaching:

- Provide ongoing professional development through online and face-to-face opportunities.

- Build in time for creating communities of practice where co-teachers may collaborate. Creating this space for co-teachers to knock down any co-teaching barriers (see the Busting Co-teaching Barriers template in the appendix) can make instructional time relevant and meaningful.

- Encourage and support teachers to make time to proactively plan and also reflect on the lessons that follow. Using the Busting Co-teaching Barriers organizer can spark this planning and reflective time.

- Provide specific feedback following ongoing walk-throughs in the classrooms. Notice the following:
  - Did both teachers take an active role in the learning process?
  - Did the students connect with both teachers?
  - Did the teachers complement each other in ways that sparked the learning for everyone?
  - Were a variety of students' needs met through the expertise of both teachers?
  - Did the teachers implement one or more co-teaching models within the time of your walk-through?
  - What went well? What would you suggest the teachers could work on?

- Create consistent classroom visits: Enter each classroom without preconceptions or expectations. Make sure the teachers know you enter judgment-free. Embrace the "We are all learners" mindset.

- Simply be curious: Be open to just being with the teachers and students. Let them feel that you are interested in being a part of their learning process.

- Keep communication open and transparent: Use shared documents, dialogue, or simply place a slip of paper in their mailbox to share:
  - What you noticed as you spent time in their room
  - What questions you have—because you are learning, too!
  - Ideas you have and connections you made that contribute to elevating their co-teaching experience

One more additional tip, for now. Yes, I saved the best for last: Administrators should enter every co-teaching partnership with a beginner's mindset. That means you exude the energy of entering each co-taught classroom as a learner yourself. You embrace your own experiences, expertise, and values—yet you remain open and enter each classroom without preconceived notions. It is a fine balance that may be achieved through keeping communication open and transparent along the way.

Yes, it always seems to come back to cultivating relationships where every member of the team values the perspectives, experiences, and expertise that each teacher, administrator, student, and parent—every member within the co-taught classroom/school community—brings to the teaching and learning process.

THE AFFECTIVE NETWORK IS THE STARTING POINT

At this point you may begin to feel the flow of the human side of co-teaching—the intangible qualities that teachers and administrators need to shine a light on as they increase their self- and collective awareness for meaningful co-teaching experiences. The next sections share two methods that administrators may implement to heighten and widen co-teaching effectiveness: the UDL learning walk and the Story in Story (SiS) approach. Both methods place the affective network front and center.

I emphasize the affective network because we need to focus on motivating administrators and teams of teachers, students, and parents to work together to increase their knowledge and understanding of the ways UDL may naturally empower all learners along the teaching and learning process. Affect refers to the noncognitive experiences that include feelings, emotions, and other autonomic responses to stimuli (Ashcroft & Tiffin, 2013, p. 4). Affect is connected to the actions we take or do not take. According to Shouse (2005), affect is biologically located and experienced, but socially responsive and culturally modulated (p. 56).

Let's pause a moment. Consider the culture in your building. Teachers, are you and your colleagues motivated and engaged in improving co-teaching in meaningful ways? Administrators, where are you along the process of improving co-teaching in your school? My experiences have rested on the value of embracing all perspectives. Wherever you find yourself, let's keep improving—it is the only way! And, if you feel that all is well and you are already doing what needs to be done, the question becomes: Now what?! How can we take what you are already doing and sustain it—and keep improving upon it?

Let's take a look at UDL learning walks as one way to engage the variability that exists within our teaching and administrative teams. This process is a strong step administrators and teachers may take in shaping a strong co-teaching partnership. UDL learning walks highlight one of the tenets of the UDL philosophy: *We are all learners!*

ELEVATING CO-TEACHING THROUGH UDL LEARNING WALKS

This non-evaluative, organically embedded professional development opportunity is quite frankly one of the most powerful ways to forge a bond between administrators, co-teachers, and students as they come together as learners throughout the year. In a sentence, UDL learning walks are authentic classroom learning experiences that deepen an understanding of UDL in real time. I have adapted the approach in a variety of co-teaching settings over the past few years. A general outline for how it works includes the following steps. Keep in mind these are not sequential steps and may occur in a different order depending on the context. However, each step will be incorporated. Before reading the following general outline, it is crucial to remember that at no time are UDL learning walks to be used as a formal teacher observation. They are a learning process for and with administrators. The integrity of the walks maintains a non-evaluative experience.

Preparing for the UDL Learning Walk

- Gather a group of interested learners. This includes at least one co-taught class (two co-teachers), building administer(s), district administrator(s) (if ready to raise awareness at the district level), and interested colleagues.

- Select one person as the group's facilitator. This person should have some knowledge (basic or otherwise) of UDL, so they may guide the learning with the group. This person may be a colleague (teacher or administrator) in the building or district or one or both of the co-teachers.

- Select one co-taught classroom. It is preferable and recommended for this to be a voluntary process. Ideas to consider include: willingness of the co-teachers, co-teachers' comfort and willingness to expand their comfort zone along the co-teaching and UDL journey, grade level (perhaps there is a desired grade level to view), and any other considerations unique to each setting.

- Select the day! The co-teachers select two or three options for the visitation. They simply select the best time of day for them based on whatever components they deem important. For example, scheduling a specific lesson based on content or process—or both! Once they share the options, the UDL learning walk team selects a day and aligns their schedules.

- Co-plan and co-prep. The co-teachers outline their lesson (this is a great time to use the Planning Prompt—see Chapter 5) and prepare as usual. The facilitator meets with the co-teachers to gain insights about the lesson.

- The facilitator provides background and purpose. At least one week before the classroom visit, the facilitator will send an informational memo to provide some background knowledge on the purpose and focus of the overall process. See the template UDL Learning Walk Information Sheet in the appendix for an example that you may use or adapt to your specific situation.

The Day of the Classroom Visit

- Co-teacher check-in. The facilitator checks in with the co-teachers and their class to make sure they are ready. They support any needed last-minute details. The facilitator reminds the students (and co-teachers!) that the visitors are coming, so they can learn from and with everyone in the room.

- Prep session (5-15 minutes). The facilitator meets with the team to provide them with the general background, context, and outline of the lesson. This time also includes a review of the purpose of UDL and SDI in a co-taught classroom. In addition, it provides the team with a guided observation sheet (see the "UDL Learning Walk Guided Observation Sheet" box) so they know what to look for, notice, and question as they become part of the learning process.

- Being a part of the learning. The team spends at least 15–20 minutes being a part of the classroom learning. They use the resources provided by the facilitator to take notes. Their presence is non-evaluative as they take on the role of learners. They may participate in any aspect of the lesson and/or be a relaxed learner through observation.

▶ UDL Learning Walk Guided Observation Sheet

	OBSERVABLE ACTION (EXAMPLES OF WHAT TEACHERS AND STUDENTS DOING AND SAYING)	WHAT I THINK ABOUT THIS
Engagement		
• Learners were active and meaningful participants with choice in what or how to learn. • Both teachers were actively and meaningfully contributing to the teaching and learning process.		
• A sense of community was present with clear evidence of collaboration. • Learners had the opportunity to monitor or regulate their learning process		
Representation		
• Teachers presented the information in a variety of ways (visual, auditory, kinesthetic, multimedia). • Teachers supported students' understanding of core concepts and vocabulary with scaffolds. • Learners applied their background knowledge and actively constructed new information and expanded their understanding.		

	OBSERVABLE ACTION (EXAMPLES OF WHAT TEACHERS AND STUDENTS DOING AND SAYING)	WHAT I THINK ABOUT THIS
Action and Expression		
• Teachers guided students to organize their thinking using specific strategies.		
• Teachers applied specific strategies to guide learners to initiate, engage, and follow through with lesson activities. • Overall, students took charge of their own learning through application of specific strategies.		
• Students were encouraged to be goal oriented as they were immersed in the process of learning. • Teachers applied specific mastery feedback to guide individual and/or groups of students to self-monitor their learning process.		

And here's a handy list of guiding questions to support your learning walk:

Engagement

1. How was student choice offered in ways to guide learners toward self-sufficiency?

2. What was evidence of peer collaboration and sense of community?

3. What was one way learners were guided to self-regulate and be self-motivated to learn?

Representation

1. What options were provided for learners to perceive the information?

2. What structures or strategies guided learners to understand vocabulary and/or concepts?

3. Did students apply their background knowledge?

4. Were students actively seeking to expand their understanding?

Action and expression

1. What structures were in place to guide learners to organize their thinking?

2. What strategies were implemented to empower learners to take charge of their own learning?

3. Were learners goal-oriented with self-monitoring opportunities in place?

Following the Walk

- Debrief session. The facilitator meets with the team for a 15–30 minute debrief to review each individual's notes, questions, and ideas. The facilitator guides the conversation by aligning with UDL principles and the premise of SDI and co-teaching. It is recommended for the co-teachers to be present to answer any questions.

- Facilitator's notes. The facilitator shares the notes they took during the walk as well as notes to synthesize the ideas from the debriefing session with the team—see the "UDL Learning Walk Facilitator Notes" and "After the Debrief Notes" boxes.

▶ UDL Learning Walk Facilitator Notes

LESSON COMPONENT AND STUDENT CHARACTERISTICS	POTENTIAL BARRIER (IN CURRICULUM OR ENVIRONMENT)	POTENTIAL UDL SOLUTIONS
1. Introduction of lesson: SMART Board slide with strategy list. Students sitting in rows. Two teachers at front of class. One teacher reviewed each reading strategy (Q&A style), student raised hand, teacher called on student. Goal for lesson reviewed by teacher orally. **Student attention, information processing needs, reading and writing difficulties.**	Pacing of introduction may have been fast for students who need support with processing and attention. Complete strategy—too much on slide for students with attention or reading difficulties. Goal of lesson shared orally. ...	Students could work in groups for a quick student-led review of strategies as both teachers monitored and listened in. Strategy strips (to match SMART Board slide) could be at each group. (Engagement) Clearly post goal of lesson on board—at groups. (Engagement) ...
2. Description of station rotation: One teacher orally explained directions for station movement. Other teacher added: "And you need to bring Post-its and a pencil."	Some students responded—most students not actively participating in discussion. Students depend on teacher rather than self-regulate. Some students responded—not all.	Post visual slide with student names and station names (Representation) Post visual slide for materials needed... ask students, "What should you bring?" (Action and Expression—self-regulation)
3. Further directions: One teacher reviewed group norms by calling on students to share. (Oral group discussion with some students sharing.)		Visual anchor chart for group norms—posted in class for consistency and self-regulation.

▶ After the Debrief Notes

Thank you for allowing us to all learn and be vulnerable together! And second, for being so open, flexible, and collaborative with me on an ongoing basis—I am loving our deep, consistent reflective process!

A little background knowledge reminder: We KNOW that UDL focuses on eliminating unintentional barriers *in the curriculum and environment*—and we focus on fixing that. (When we see through a UDL lens, there is never a focus on "fixing" the child.)

OK! So . . .

In addition to the many ways you naturally embedded UDL into your classroom, here are a few more notes based on our debrief session as administrators were guided to deepen their understanding of UDL.

More Possibilities!

Principal A thought of another option for station rotation—putting a nice new spin on multiple means of action and expression. Why not have the teachers move and rotate? Could provide opportunity for deeper formative assessment, specific mastery feedback for students, and support for students to monitor their progress. (Action and Expression)

With UDL becoming a stronger presence in your classroom, we stretch our thinking and pave the way for specially designed instruction (more specific, proactive differentiation) for specific students. For example, the UDL strategies in place worked for students who struggle with writing. They selected a graphic organizer that allowed them to focus on going deeper in their writing. With UDL creating the access for most students in the class, we can see those who need more—like Samantha. We will follow up with specific strategies to further support them (specially designed instruction—deeper differentiation). (Action and Expression, Engagement)

Bravo! The graphic organizer choice was a natural scaffold that supported writers who struggle and writers who needed more of a challenge. Those who needed a challenge selected the newest graphic organizer—just recently introduced, for example. (Engagement)

The station groups fostered a sense of community and collaboration (Engagement)

I LOVE coming into your classroom and being a part of the community that we create together—thank you for being open, flexible, and collaborative. And having you, Principal A, as a part of this journey expands all possibilities!

Let's keep the communication going—please add questions, comments, or anything on your mind to keep our learning moving forward . . . together!

UDL learning walks are highly individualized within the context of each district, school building, classroom, and team of educators involved in the experience. The facilitator has the responsibility to support the learning for each team member by honoring the group's individual perspectives. The facilitator should be someone connected to the co-teaching classroom in some way and comfortable taking on the role in a way that honors that they, too, are part of the learning process. They remain open to learning as they listen to the perspectives of others, connect with their knowledge of co-teaching and UDL, and then expand ideas while honoring each team member's understanding of UDL.

UDL learning walks create opportunities for the facilitator and the team to describe the affective nature of co-teaching. Honoring individual perspectives within a team approach brings us to the next idea administrators may apply as they support co-teaching experiences.

ELEVATING CO-TEACHING THROUGH A STORY IN STORY (SiS) APPROACH

The Story in Story (SiS) approach is another uniquely effective step administrators may take to encourage the joint efforts and shared experiences of co-teachers, parents, and students. I created the SiS approach to illuminate the way multiple perspectives interact to inform the instructional decisions of the two co-teachers under study (Stein, 2021); that is, I created it as a method for identifying, organizing, and applying the viewpoints within my analysis process. I immediately found the approach valuable as a practitioner as well. Simultaneously, I adapted the approach as I worked with teachers and administrators in the field.

My hope is that the simple structure of SiS implementation will result in a wide range of possibilities for how this approach will work in each unique situation. I see the approach as a way for an administrator to guide authentic and organic solutions both in response to co-teaching trouble spots and as a proactive collaborative activity to knock down possible barriers to the co-teaching and co-learning process. Before sharing the general outline for implementation, let's take a look at an example of the SiS approach in action.

SiS Scenario #1

At his request, I met with the principal on a cool October day. I happened to arrive as students were going to their lockers, bustling to make it to their next class before the bell rang. He explained his concern as "a very difficult situation because it is only October, and we have the whole year ahead of us." He continued to share that he was not used to having to get involved with co-teachers at the high school level. "We have tried everything, yet [this co-teacher] just keeps pushing the buttons of every co-teacher—every period. I just don't know what to do. At least once a day for the past two weeks, teachers have been coming to me to complain." After I listened to further details, we both agreed that my next step would be to meet with the special educator.

I met her in her classroom the next day. The 20-minute session was spent with me listening. This teacher shared her frustration with "the way they do things here." She explained her efforts in trying to co-plan and co-teach as well as co-assess in each content-area class she was assigned. "These teachers just don't play nice. And I am just supposed to accept that. Well, I can't do that—I made a promise to my students the second I agreed to take this position."

When I asked her to elaborate on what she meant by "they don't play nice," she explained the lack of communication and, most important, the lack of trust she felt they had in her. Her bottom line was "for the most part they just don't give me a chance to do what is right for our students." I noticed when she said "our students," she added an emphasis on the word *our*. Following that meeting, I spent about 10 minutes with each of the general educators on this co-teaching team. One revealed, "Things are going well. I am getting used to her way. She is not like any other special educator I've worked with—she shares a lot of her own ideas and that can be a good thing." The other three general educators individually shared a common theme. "She just tries too hard—really all we need her to do is help her kids." Each teacher shared additional information connected to their specific content area.

Role delineation, time management, and view of educating students with disabilities were clear barriers in guiding a smooth co-teaching process. I decided to apply the SiS approach as I met with the administrator two days later. The SiS approach allowed me to show him, rather than tell him, how I interpreted and identified the problem. The SiS diagram I created is shown in Figure 10.1. Names have been removed for confidentiality purposes. I chose to share this story by identifying the role each teacher played to guide readers' reflections.

When the principal viewed the SiS diagram, he released the paper on his desk as he took off his glasses. As the paper quickly floated to rest on the desk, he sat back, smiled, and then looked out the window. "I was so busy trying to fix this current situation that I never stopped to consider the past experiences or even the way these teachers view their own role in educating students in these [co-taught] classrooms."

Special educator

"My other district supported co-teachers by providing consistent planning time and holding everyone accountable. Here, co-teachers just xerox or email their plans to me, but there is never a discussion about it."

General educator: Math

"Oh, I think everything is okay. We meet every day for five minutes before class starts to review the lesson and how we will teach it."

General educator: Science

"It's going okay. She emails me a lot with some good ideas, and I use the ideas for the most part—it's good. It's just that this period is the only period I co-teach and do something different, and I worry that we do not have time for some of these ideas."

General educator: Social studies

"She is just distracting to my teaching. The students don't know who to listen to or who to look at sometimes. The other day, for example, she was modeling note-taking on the board as I was teaching. Every special educator I ever worked with just stayed quiet and helped their kids when they needed it."

General educator: English

"Honestly, she makes me twitch. I get nervous when she shares an idea or comes to me and says how about we try this or that. But I like her ideas, and I think she makes more kids in class participate, so I am willing to try some new things. I just get nervous because I don't want to run out of time teaching the material I need to teach."

FIGURE 10.1. SiS scenario #1—problem to solve: honoring and expanding each co-teacher's view about co-teaching

In dialogue with the principal, we came up with the following focal points to discuss with the teachers as a group:

- All students are "our" students.

- Make time to review what and how to teach together.

- Value the expertise of each co-teacher (the special educator and the general educator).

- Make sure each co-teacher is an active part of the teaching and learning process before, during, and after every lesson.

- Understand students with disabilities are a part of—not a subgroup within—the whole group of variable learners.

The essence of UDL reveals honoring the unique and varied ways learners perceive information, engage in the act of learning, and express their understanding of specific subject matter. The SiS approach honors the educators through this same lens by valuing their varied experiences, perspectives, and expertise. Each co-teacher in this case brought their individual belief system to the classroom every day. The science teacher, for example, expressed frustration in trying to teach all periods in the same way. He struggled with the reality that the co-taught classroom needed a different approach while valuing the abilities of every learner. He also struggled with relinquishing some time to his co-teacher to teach; rather, he takes her ideas and teaches them himself, as she is expected to quietly walk around the room monitoring student learning. The social studies teacher revealed his efforts to be *the* teacher while creating an attitudinal barrier with the aim of keeping the special educator as a quiet "helper" in the room. The math teacher revealed an open mind in acknowledging the value of consistent communication and co-planning time. The English teacher was honest in sharing that he felt nervous yet, at the same time, curious about the new teaching ideas the special educator shared.

The principal and I decided to share the SiS diagram with the group during a 20-minute discussion. The revealing nature of authentic quotes and perspectives from each co-teacher created a visual icebreaker to help expand the co-teaching mindset in the group. As a result of this SiS discussion, the special educator was asked by the principal to explain a bit more about her past co-teaching experiences. Before the SiS discussion, this group did not consider how their past experiences influenced their beliefs about what co-teaching should look like in their classrooms. Using the personalized SiS diagram, the group came up with their next steps as they considered the multiple perspectives shared and embraced by each teacher. It was certainly not going to be a quick fix; however, it was the start of a new process where each co-teacher stepped beyond the boundaries of their own view and began to consider and value the perspectives of one another. This new, united entry point created new opportunities and possibilities for elevating their co-teaching experience.

The next example demonstrates the value of including the explicit perspective of students along the process of co-creating a culture of belonging in their classroom. Once again, this example was adapted from the structure of my SiS approach (Stein, 2021).

SiS Scenario #2

The special education teacher shared her frustration with "a few students in this seventh-grade class who just like to cause trouble. They refuse to do any work; they often call out in ways that distract the flow of whole-class lessons. In addition, they just don't seem to care." During a recent informal visit from the principal, these three students "acted out by laughing and calling out during the lesson even more than usual."

The co-teachers agreed to plan a class that involved small-group work during class time. Each co-teacher facilitated a group, while I facilitated a brief discussion with the three students to gain insights into how they were experiencing school—and this class in particular. We rotated every 10 minutes, so every student rotated through each small-group activity. I launched this time together by simply asking, "How is school going for you?" Receiving generic responses of "It's good," "It's boring," "I don't really know," I followed the vibe and got right to it: "How is everything going in this class?" All three students shifted from slouching in their seats to sitting up a bit taller. They chimed right in: "It's the best class," "Yeah, it's good but can be frustrating sometimes," "It's the only class where we are all together—the rest of the day, we don't get to see each other until after school." Bingo! I learned so much in that three-second response. The organic process of dialogue unfolded. I invited them to elaborate on their feelings simply by stating: "Oh, I would love to hear more about that." Or, "Tell us more about that." At points I probed with more specificity, such as: "What makes you feel frustrated?" I served as an active listener for the remaining seven minutes. I noticed that each of the three students not only shared their thoughts but also listened, supported, and responded to one another. It was clear their friendship was well established. The SiS diagram in Figure 10.2 shows the SiS approach in action to reveal multiple perspectives. After I shared the students' responses with the teachers, they agreed to each meet with me for five minutes. During this time, I simply asked each, "What do you think about the students' responses? What do you think your role is in their current perspective?" I also asked: "What could you personally do differently to honor the perspective of the students?" With the permission of the co-teachers, I also spoke with the principal, who had recently observed the class, and I added his view to the SiS discussion diagram.

Students
- "This is the only class we have together and the only time we see each other all day."
- "Class is good, but it can be frustrating because Mr. H. does a lot of talking."
- "It is frustrating because we have to just sit and listen to the teacher talk."
- "We get in trouble a lot just because we are trying to have some fun. What's wrong with having fun, anyway?"

Special educator
"I feel bad because I know there is more that I can do. Even though these are not all classified students, everyone needs support in note-taking. I know my ideas for teaching are so different from [my co-teacher's], and it can be uncomfortable. I agree with the kids—there is too much talking. I even get bored in the class. Honestly, I don't blame them. I want to be more active in the teaching process."

Principal
"This is a common problem with a not-so-easy solution. Co-teaching is not always easy. These two have to find a better balance to reach the kids. It always bothers me when one co-teacher is doing most of the heavy lifting and is turned off by including the other."

General educator
"I provide a lot of visuals, and my talking is necessary to explain all of that. They have to learn to listen better, and the visuals should help that. Most of the class follows along, so I don't know what else I can do for these students. They have to do their part."

FIGURE 10.2. SiS scenario #2—problem to solve: student behaviors distracting during instructional time

The final step in this SiS approach was to gather everyone together for a debrief discussion. The principal organized a common time, and everyone agreed to meet. I shared the SiS discussion diagram with everyone. The first minute of the meeting was dedicated to silence as each member read through the varying perspectives. The principal and I then facilitated a productive conversation that was organic in nature. We discussed the value of each person's perspective as I emphasized the awareness that as each person held their view, there were other stories—other perspectives—happening at the same time. Each story—each person's feelings—should be valued and included as decisions were being made to solve the problem of disruptive behavior. As a result of this principal-facilitated conversation, the following solutions were agreed upon:

- The principal would create time in the co-teachers' schedules for co-planning time.

- The special educator would share note-taking strategies as well as other strategies that provided alternatives to the general educator lecturing alongside visuals.

- The general educator would also share new ideas for teaching techniques and remain open to new ways of teaching and learning.

- The principal would visit the classroom at least once each week and be a part of the process of growth with the group.

- The students would become more aware of how their behaviors affect everyone's learning. They agreed if they could sit together, they would not call out, laugh, and engage in other distracting behaviors.

- It was also agreed by all that as the co-teachers worked together to include more engaging teaching techniques, the students would be too busy participating in the activities to act out in a distracting manner.

- Each person agreed to remain accountable for their part toward improving the classroom learning environment. They would keep communication open throughout the weeks and meet as a group as needed.

In the spirit of UDL, I am pleased to introduce you to the next strategy, which also encourages co-teaching teams to honor multiple perspectives. I call it the co-teaching universe strategy, adapted from Freire's (1970) idea of a thematic universe and the discovery of the vocabulary universe (Freire & Macedo, 2005). Freire emphasized the basic premise of generating words in dialogue with others as a way toward social transformation by illuminating the reality of each individual within the community.

THE CO-TEACHING UNIVERSE

I reinvented Freire's thematic universe (1970, 2007) and created the co-teaching universe strategy as a way to bring the human side of education to the forefront of any co-teaching and learning process. The co-teaching universe strategy may be applied between two co-teachers, or it may be elevated by including principals and other stakeholders in the midst of an illuminating and empowering process of co-creating powerful co-taught experiences. The generated words become the tool for multiple means of representation and transformation of the world of co-teaching as individuals express words that are authentic to their lived experiences and their interpretations of the words in their co-teaching experiences.

This strategy aims to elevate and deepen meaningful co-teaching in humanizing ways—not the mechanistic, lockstep ways that often result from following checklists and procedures. This strategy guides relationships through an organic, dialogic process. In the following sidebar I share a general structure with the understanding that the process should unfold as needed depending on the team and the context; through this relational connection, co-teachers and team members may work to improve accordingly. I then share two examples based on my own personal experiences and vision for how this strategy may unfold.

▶ The Co-teaching Universe Strategy

Goal:

To create a culture of trust, respect, ongoing communication, and meaningful action steps within co-teaching teams

Process:

1. **Beginning stage.** One person is designated the lead facilitator, with the knowledge that everyone is a co-facilitator along the process. The lead facilitator is needed to document the list of words that are clearly visible for everyone to see. Words may be documented on a shared Google Doc, large digital screen, or chart paper. In addition, the lead facilitator will insert guided questions as needed to keep the group on track. Questions should be general and may include:

    - How is co-teaching going so far this year?
    - What is working well?
    - What needs improvement?

2. **Discovery stage.** Members create a list of 18 words that create space to discuss beliefs embraced by co-teachers and other members of

the team toward transforming any co-teaching experience. The list of authentic words must come from the individuals in the group to express the way they see their reality of co-teaching. This personal list of words will express their preoccupations, intentions, anxieties, frustrations, dreams, and hopes. This list becomes the focus for individual and collective interpretations toward co-creating solutions and other actions needed for meaningful co-teaching experiences.

3. **Interpretative stage.** At this stage the learning begins as individuals reflect, then connect with their interpretations of the generated words.

4. **Dialogic stage.** The individuals share their interpretations of the words. This stage begins to transcend words as they start taking the shape of expanded views through individual and collective actions.

Example A: The Principal Scratches His Head in Confusion

The principal hears rumblings about co-teachers having problems within their classrooms. After a few weeks, he realizes there is a problem—it does not seem to be just rumors. He thinks, *I just don't get it. During observations I see co-teachers are working well together and the students clearly respect and make good use of having two teachers. I provide common planning time, and I even walk around often and pop into their classrooms informally with a smile at least once per week or every two weeks. I am present—and they know it. Why am I hearing about these problems secondhand?*

The principal decides to make this a topic of discussion at the next faculty meeting. He dedicates 15 minutes to the co-teaching universe strategy. He strategically asks co-teachers to sit in the same area within the large auditorium. In addition, he guides grade-level teachers to sit near each other as well, with the intention of promoting rich grade-level conversations. This part of the meeting begins as the principal shares his view and positive experiences observing and walking through classrooms and makes it clear that he wants to learn more by finding out how it is going from each teacher's perspective. The discovery stage begins as the whole group brainstorms 18 words. This stage is simply sparked, in this context, when the principal asks the question: "How is co-teaching going?" As teachers call out words, the principal enters the words on a document displayed on the large screen for all to see. It takes three minutes for the group to share 18 words. The list of words looks like this:

lesson plans	attention	disposition
manage	time	windows
pencils	visual models	small groups
desks	laptops	co-teaching models
rows	parents	change
textbooks	phone calls	past experiences

Following the exercise, the principal asks, "Are we in agreement? Are there any words you would like to delete? Add? Change in any way?" He then asks the teachers to work in smaller groups for five to eight minutes to interpret and engage in dialogue about their interpretations. As the groups discuss, the principal walks around the large auditorium and gathers comments in his notebook. Here are some examples of comments he gathers:

- "The visual models are distracting. As I am teaching and you are sharing visual models, the students just stop paying attention to me and are just looking at what you are doing."

- "You just have many past experiences with co-teaching and this is all new for me, and it is hard."

- "You manage classroom routines and behaviors very differently from me, and it is hard for me to know my role in supporting this when I have a different philosophy."

- "It is hard to change the way I am used to teaching."

- "I am afraid of running out of time to teach all that I am responsible to teach if I have to share instructional time with another teacher."

- "Visual models are a great addition to the lessons. I just wish I had the plans to the lessons so I can plan ahead and not always have to teach on the fly."

- "Pencils remind me of the many ways the students are unprepared."

- "I wish we could balance our teaching styles—I want to bring the textbook alive, not just have the kids read robotically to answer questions."

The principal reads through some of the comments. He adds them to the document that presents the 18 words. He spends the remaining time reminding the group of the value of multiple perspectives. A word means one thing to one person and something different to another. Our views must be shared if we want co-teaching to be meaningful.

Example B: Two Teachers Picking Up the Pieces

This was the first time these two teachers co-taught together. It has been many years since the general educator shared his classroom. Although the special educator is used to co-teaching for the past 10 years, she is tired of the need to "start from square one" every year. Just when she adapts to working with one co-teacher, the process begins all over again. The first few months were uneventful.

Then came December. The principal approached the team to inform them she received a few calls from parents with a few complaints. The principal was supportive and worked it out with the teachers. The principal returned the parent phone calls with the solutions in place and was happy to hear that the parents felt the problems were resolved as well. Although the teachers were happy to hear this, they couldn't help but feel there were still underlying issues between them.

They decided to spend time during their next co-planning session engaging in the co-teaching universe strategy. They spent the first few minutes writing an individual list of 18 words to respond to how they were experiencing co-teaching together. They then shared their individual lists by first transferring all similar words to their shared list. They then discussed each remaining word on each list and decided which words to add to their shared list.

They decided to keep their individual lists for further conversations another time. The shared list looked like this:

leader	assessments	parents
talk	lesson planning	rotations
lessons	classroom routines	motivation
answer key	behavior plan	skills
co-teaching models	sunshine	strategies
goals	flexibility	homework

Their conversation opened up to include:

- "I wish we could vary the co-teaching models—some lessons would work better with different ways to structure and present the materials."
- "We basically use the team-teach approach, and I do not always feel comfortable jumping in. I am not always doing what I feel is best for the students."
- "Maybe if we rotate parent phone calls or call together, we can improve more open communication with the parents."
- "Some kids are using the answer key before doing the work. I have an idea that would motivate them to do the thinking they need to do first."
- "My goals for teaching and your goals for teaching feel like two different entities—we have to align both worlds, so we do all we can together for these students."
- "If they don't do their homework, that is on them; there isn't anything we can do."
- "How about if we assign more meaningful homework and add a little choice to the mix?"

They shared this time by expressing their interpretations with a hint of some types of actions they could take to improve their co-teaching experience. They decided to share their co-teaching universe activity with the principal. She was now a part of the team and ready to dig deeper in the ways she supported this team.

KEY TAKEAWAYS

✔ There are a variety of ways administrators and co-teachers may sustain ongoing partnerships throughout the year to elevate any co-teaching experience.

✔ When administrators enter a co-taught classroom with a beginner's mindset, they become a part of the learning community with the philosophy: *We are all learners.* Through this non-evaluative, welcoming manner, a strong connection may be established.

✔ UDL learning walks, the Story in Story (SiS) approach (Stein, 2021), and the co-teaching universe are three meaningful ways to elevate co-teaching with administrators as partners.

STUDY GROUP QUESTIONS

1. As you review the tips for administrators, what is one tip you believe you may encourage with your administrator tomorrow?

2. How could UDL learning walks be applied in your school?

3. When we apply a SiS approach, we are valuing the perspective of all co-teaching partners. How do you see this approach benefiting you, your co-teacher, and your students?

4. What is another tip or strategy you learned in this chapter that you feel excited about?

11

Never Stop Elevating!
Reflections and Next Steps

THE UDL JOURNEY is a unique experience for everyone. Yet partnering with colleagues, students, parents, and administrators expands our personal perspective in ways that can create equitable and meaningful learning experiences. A UDL mindset is achieved when UDL feels naturally embedded in the instructional planning, implementation, and assessment cycles—when it does not feel like "one more thing." It is a process that should not be rushed; it comes in time, through collaboration. It is never something separate or added on to a lesson. At first it will likely feel like more work since you are required to become more mindful of your applications. With time, however, it will feel like a natural cycle of meaningful learning where all learners in the room are active participants as thinkers, speakers, and listeners who flow through multiple means of learning opportunities that optimize personal achievements.

The implementation of the UDL Guidelines may feel like a checklist to accomplish, but with practice, it becomes an organic flow of learning as it weaves naturally through your instructional decisions and applications. Students and teachers respond positively to this stimulating learning environment because all thinking is valued; all students feel the presence of opportunities to personally connect to the curriculum. UDL naturally flows within meaningful learning experiences that truly strengthen each student's relationship with themselves as learners.

Once this UDL lens is established, co-teachers begin to communicate in ways that value how students are grappling with the content—not just keeping a focus on the outcome as an endpoint but rather as a process of ongoing learning and achieving. Co-teachers should discuss and co-plan the ways to design lessons so that the content is accessible to all students as well as rigorous in that it creates personal connections and deeper learning. For example, Joey is an eighth-grade student who is reading on a sixth-grade reading level. Here's what a quick co-teaching debrief during a low-tech UDL lesson could look like:

> TEACHER 1: "I think that lesson on Reconstruction went well—all students had the opportunity to access the reading we needed them to accomplish."
>
> TEACHER 2: "Yes, I agree! Joey was able to maintain his focus because we created the option for the students to view the video at station #1—that really provided the background knowledge they all needed. And it helped Joey to connect what we were learning with what he already knows about the Civil War."
>
> TEACHER 1: "And when it came time to the reading, I am so glad we didn't have the students just read silently at their seats. Setting up the options for some to read silently, others to read in small groups, and yet others to join one of us in a more guided reading experience really made the difference!"
>
> TEACHER 2: "Yes, I'm glad Joey chose to read with his peers in the small group. He really followed along, and he was the perfect note-taker for the group."

With a UDL lens, the focus is on teachers reflecting on their instructional decisions to create clear access between each learner in the room and the content itself. In this example, Joey's reading level was a barrier to his accessing the material on his own. Yet, through proactive planning, the co-teachers worked together to create a process that allowed for the material to reach learners in a variety of ways.

REVISITING CLASSROOM SCENARIOS

In Chapter 4, we looked at two classrooms where teachers implemented the same lesson in very different ways.

What was your first impression? Did both classrooms apply effective instruction? Be specific—explain why you think the way you do. Are you able to identify the co-teaching models of instruction that each co-teaching pair applies? Are you able to identify the UDL components? You had some time to think about it. Feel free to look through this book to refresh and strengthen your voice as you begin to put specific language into describing what was happening in each classroom. Let's refresh our memories.

Co-taught Classroom #1
(Any Grade, Any Subject, Anywhere)

Focus Anchor Standard: Determine central ideas or themes of a text and analyze their development; summarize the key supporting details and ideas.

The class of 25 students is sitting in rows listening to one of the teachers reading aloud from a chapter book. The teacher walks up and down the rows as she dramatically reads and makes eye contact with each student. She uses her voice to guide students to visualize character traits and story elements. She pauses every so often to remind students to close their eyes and visualize. There are no external visuals. There are no additional materials. Just one teacher, rows of desks, and students sitting at their desks encouraged using their imaginations. The students are visibly attentive as they watch the teacher read with some dramatic displays of expression and voice. A few chuckles can be heard around the room as she reads. The second co-teacher is at the back of the room; he is following along in his copy of the book, ready to take over the reading as the first teacher nods and smiles his way. Before this second teacher reads, he asks the students a few guided questions to make sure they are following along and understanding what's happening in the text so far. These questions are orally presented to the entire class. There are no visuals and no additional materials. The students are still sitting in their seats. This teacher also walks around the room, so all of the students are once again seemingly attentive. A few students eagerly raise their hands. A few students quickly look down at their shoes as the teacher walks past their desk. One or two students are called on, the answers to the comprehension questions are revealed, and the teacher succinctly sums up what has happened in the reading so far. He is ready to continue reading. Students once again follow the teacher's movements and smile as he, too, reads with dramatic expression. At the end of the reading, the first teacher says, "Great class today! Be ready for a quiz on this chapter at the beginning of our next class." The teacher quickly directs the class to transition to the next subject.

Co-taught Classroom #2

The class of 25 students is sitting in groups of five. Students' desks are facing one another. The first teacher is up at the SMART Board reviewing some active reading strategies. She opens a discussion on how to annotate the text to deepen the readers' comprehension. The second co-teacher takes the lead and tells the class they will be practicing this annotation skill during the reading of a short paragraph, as he models his thinking and annotating.

The first co-teacher asks each group to discuss what they noticed about the teacher's think-aloud and how it connected to their own thinking. Students are given a few minutes to discuss. Following a quick debriefing, the first co-teacher introduces the text they are about to read. She offers students a choice. They can read the text while following along with text-to-speech software, they can engage in a shared reading with one of the teachers reading aloud, they can use iPads to read the text electronically with the use of dictionary apps, they can partner-read with a peer, or they can choose to go solo and read silently. This may sound like a lot of choices, but these students are used to making decisions for how they will learn best. Their opinions, feelings, moods, and voice are valued each day.

The classroom is set up for the ease of arranging desks and the flexibility for students to choose the process for engaging in the learning experience. As the students move seamlessly around the room, all are ready to begin the reading task within a few minutes. The teachers do not need to assign student groups. Thirteen students choose to go solo and complete the reading assignment successfully on their own while using the iPads occasionally to support their vocabulary knowledge. Five students sit in a group with one of the co-teachers reading as they follow along. Two students choose to partner-read, while five students choose to go to the computer lab where the librarian has set them up to read along using Google text-to-speech supports. The other co-teacher is monitoring the engagement of all students and implementing supports as needed. He notices that all students are engaged and taking charge of their own learning.

Let's Discuss!

Now, look back at what you wrote down as your first impressions in Chapter 4. Are you able to add to your thoughts now? How has your thinking about UDL and co-teaching changed after reading this book? Harvard education professor Richard F. Elmore (2011) developed a professional development protocol called "I used to think . . . and now I think . . ." that can be helpful here.

Complete these sentences:

I used to think UDL was _____. Now I think _____.

I used to think co-teaching was _____. Now I think
_____.

UDL can elevate instruction in inclusive classrooms with co-teachers when
_____.

Now that you have a deeper sense of your co-teaching with UDL stance, let's take a look at the two classrooms we just entered. Keep in mind, anything I share here is just my ideas—there are no right or wrong responses in our UDL reflections. It's just important to get the conversations started and the collaborations going and going.

So, let's begin!

Evidence of Effective Instruction in Both Classrooms

Classroom #1

Teachers use their voice and eye contact to connect and engage learners. One of the teachers stopped to summarize key points and allowed learners time to process what was happening so far in the text.

Classroom #2

Students are in groups rather than in rows. This seating arrangement encourages peer interactions and collaboration. Cooperative learning activities were planned with the learners at the center of the instruction. They are provided choices, time to process, time to move, time to collaborate, and time to engage in meaningful tasks that align with the learning goals. All learners are supported in ways that challenge them while supporting their thinking and learning to move beyond the point where they started. Technology was used in effective ways to support learning opportunities.

Evidence of Co-teaching Models

Classroom #1

One may argue that this is team teaching because teachers are technically teaching together—they each have a role, and they are both active. Another may argue this is one teaches, one assists, because as one teacher leads the class, the other is somewhere in the room—hopefully monitoring students' performance in some way. And yet another may argue that there is not a clearly defined co-teaching model at all. It could appear that these teachers are just taking turns. If taking turns is the case, then co-teachers, beware! Do not fall into the taking-turns trap. Ask yourself, *Is there any specialized instruction going on? Is there evidence that the special education teacher has embedded some strategies to support learning?* In classroom #1, there is some evidence that the second teacher included processing time to summarize and review key points. But is that enough? You be the judge.

Classroom #2

This seems to be team teaching at its best! Both teachers introduce the lesson, model strategic thinking, and allow students time to collaborate and process in meaningful ways to allow each to personally connect. In addition, once students move into groups of their choice, they are all working toward the same high standards, but they are given the opportunity to engage in the learning process in ways that support and challenge them to learn the material. One co-teacher facilitates the learning in a small group, while the other teacher monitors the whole class and supports as needed. This could be viewed as the workshop model, allowing students to apply strategies taught to them. This is clearly a positive learning environment for all.

Evidence of UDL Components

Classroom #1

- *Engagement*: Teachers use their voice and facial expressions. One teacher embeds time to process and monitor comprehension through summarizing key points.

- *Representation*: The material is primarily presented through an auditory modality with some visual as the teachers display the reading in dramatic ways.

- *Action and expression*: The method is whole-class discussion through oral expression, which may leave many students behind if auditory processing is not a strength. In addition, all students will be given a quiz during the next class. But ask yourself, *Was each learner supported to comprehend the text?*

Classroom #2

- *Engagement*: The use of resources is varied to optimize learning. Peer collaboration is fostered as well as students' abilities to reflect and connect with the learning process.

- *Representation*: Learning is supported through guided scaffolds to increase comprehension and extend background knowledge. Alternatives to auditory and visual information were naturally embedded.

- *Action and expression*: Methods of actions and responses are varied through the use of multiple media. Students' strategic thinking was supported through a variety of tools and technologies. Students were given the opportunities to monitor their learning by allowing them to make choices and monitor their comprehension and performance throughout the learning experience.

WRAPPING UP

The greatest part about coming to the end of this book is that there really is no end. Sure, this is the last page of the final chapter, but it is the beginning of you launching or continuing your learning and practical application process. You can acknowledge and intentionally relax into the reassuring thought that deciding to embrace a UDL mindset is a process—and I am here for you every step of the way. It takes time and commitment to an open-minded learning process. It is really a beginning. You have many options here. You may go back and reread sections of the text, engage in the co-teaching check-in activities, and put sticky notes on pages that resonate and reveal the strategies you want to implement with your co-teacher, students, and school community. Perhaps you will keep the book close by as a ready reference and ongoing support to guide you in bringing your co-teaching experiences to the most effective levels as you move along your own expert learner path. The most important next step you can make is the decision to see how UDL may elevate your relationships, your knowledge, and your instructional decisions throughout all of your co-teaching and collaborative action steps ahead. In the spirit of UDL, my hope is that reading this book will become an iterative process that leads you through a learning loop and keeps you inquiring about the information shared, making responsible decisions for implementing what you've learned, and engaging in discussions and reflections for beginning the learning loop all over again as you plan and co-plan learning experiences throughout the year.

The Universal Design for Learning Guidelines

CAST | Until learning has no limits

Provide multiple means of Engagement
Affective Networks
The "WHY" of Learning

Provide multiple means of Representation
Recognition Networks
The "WHAT" of Learning

Provide multiple means of Action & Expression
Strategic Networks
The "HOW" of Learning

Access

Provide options for Recruiting Interest
- Optimize individual choice and autonomy
- Optimize relevance, value, and authenticity
- Minimize threats and distractions

Provide options for Perception
- Offer ways of customizing the display of information
- Offer alternatives for auditory information
- Offer alternatives for visual information

Provide options for Physical Action
- Vary the methods for response and navigation
- Optimize access to tools and assistive technologies

Build

Provide options for Sustaining Effort & Persistence
- Heighten salience of goals and objectives
- Vary demands and resources to optimize challenge
- Foster collaboration and community
- Increase mastery-oriented feedback

Provide options for Language & Symbols
- Clarify vocabulary and symbols
- Clarify syntax and structure
- Support decoding of text, mathematical notation, and symbols
- Promote understanding across languages
- Illustrate through multiple media

Provide options for Expression & Communication
- Use multiple media for communication
- Use multiple tools for construction and composition
- Build fluencies with graduated levels of support for practice and performance

Internalize

Provide options for Self Regulation
- Promote expectations and beliefs that optimize motivation
- Facilitate personal coping skills and strategies
- Develop self-assessment and reflection

Provide options for Comprehension
- Activate or supply background knowledge
- Highlight patterns, critical features, big ideas, and relationships
- Guide information processing and visualization
- Maximize transfer and generalization

Provide options for Executive Functions
- Guide appropriate goal-setting
- Support planning and strategy development
- Facilitate managing information and resources
- Enhance capacity for monitoring progress

Goal

Expert learners who are...

| Purposeful & Motivated | Resourceful & Knowledgeable | Strategic & Goal-Directed |

udlguidelines.cast.org | © CAST, Inc. 2018 | Suggested Citation: CAST (2018). Universal design for learning guidelines version 2.2 [graphic organizer]. Wakefield, MA: Author.

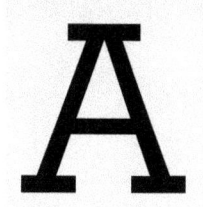

Appendix

IN THE FOLLOWING PAGES, YOU'LL find templates and resources referenced throughout the book. We hope you'll find them helpful. They are, in order of reference:

Chapter 1

Co-teaching Shared Vision Planning Page

Example Letter Showing Co-teachers' Communication with Principals

Principal to Co-teachers Check-in

Chapter 2

Class Learning Profile Template

Class Learning Profile Sample

Chapter 4

Student Application Cue Card

Teacher Modeling Cue Card

Chapter 5

Busting Co-teaching Barriers

Strengths-based Check-in Reflection

Chapter 6

Letter to Learners

Letter to Parents and Caregivers

Chapter 7

Scan–Question–Read–Write Template

Chapter 10

UDL Learning Walk Information Sheet

Teachers: _____   School Year: _____

Co-teaching Shared Vision Planning Page

Get your co-teaching year off to a strong start by sharing your views and then combining them into one shared vision for the year. Each co-teacher should write his or her response to each of the key questions. Once this page is complete, be sure to view this shared vision throughout the year so that you strengthen your co-actions and stay on track.

	Co-teacher:	Co-teacher:
Name a few variables that support students' learning.		
What is your view on the optimal classroom learning environment?		
What talents do you bring as a teacher that you know can maximize the learning process for your students?		
What is the best way to address students' learning differences?		

Combined Shared Vision:

© 2016 Elizabeth Stein

FIGURE A.1. Co-teaching Shared Vision Planning Page

Dear _____:

All co-teaching experiences range on a continuum between very awkward and unsuccessful to extremely cooperative, collaborative, and successful. All co-teaching experiences fall somewhere along this continuum of success. As you know, we are ready to do all we can to fall at the very successful end of the continuum. Yet we cannot do this alone. You can do a few things to support us as we strive to make this the most positive experience for our students and for ourselves.

Creating a Building-Wide View of Variable Learners

Let's work together to redirect the thoughts that there are two teachers in the room because "some" students need extra help. Let's reframe these mindsets and create a school culture where students, teachers, and parents accept that all learners are variable learners. Students with disabilities are part of this natural variability. Learner variability acknowledges that there is no such thing as the average learner—there is only variability. Let's support all students and not single any student out. This variability may be proactively planned for by designing instruction to meet the needs of each learner through using the UDL Guidelines as a framework for organizing our instruction so that each student may not only access the curriculum, but also meaningful connect, process, and apply their understandings.

Creating a Culture of Collaboration

Let's make it a priority for us to have time to co-plan, to debrief, and to reflect. Each student in our room needs both of us to be on the same page. In addition, we need this co-planning time to work out any bumps in the road that will inevitably arise. In addition to our personal collaboration time, we need to connect with our colleagues. Let's find ways to naturally embed time for us to connect with other colleagues and support staff.

© 2016 Elizabeth Stein

FIGURE A.2. Example Letter Showing Co-teachers' Communication with Principals

Be a Part of our Team

We need you to be a part of our process. Please visit us in our classroom. Share your thoughts on what you notice in the classroom. What are we doing well? How can we improve? Your presence, support, and knowledge of our students and class routines will serve to empower us as we meet with any stumbling blocks along the way. Please use the Principal to Co-teachers Check-in to provide us with specific, objective feedback. We need this objective view!

Let's keep the communication open so that all of us remain focused and active along the path toward a successful co-teaching year! Thank you for all of your support.

Sincerely,

© 2016 Elizabeth Stein

FIGURE A.2 CONT. Example Letter Showing Co-teachers' Communication with Principals

Principal to Co-teachers Check-in

Co-teachers: _____ Principal: _____ Date: _____

This check-in is nonevaluative. The purpose is to guide both teachers toward strong parity and clearly defined roles in order to create a positive co-teaching environment. Each mark placed on the continuum for each question signifies what was noticed for this unannounced, quick check-in. The completed check-in should be used to guide the co-teachers in their professional growth, collaboration, and ultimately each student's personal achievements.

1. Both teachers were actively part of the learning process.

| One teacher dominated while the other teacher quietly walked around the room. | Both teachers were active with clear, visible, roles. |

2. Students were engaged. This was evident because students were actively speaking, moving, and/or demonstrating their understanding.

| Students were passively sitting at their seats for the most part. | Student voice and choice was evident. |

© 2016 Elizabeth Stein

FIGURE A.3. Principal to Co-teachers Check-in

3. Instruction was clearly designed around the UDL principles with additional scaffolds to support students' IEP goals through specially designed instruction.

Instruction was designed primarily around the curriculum. No evidence of UDL or co-teaching with SDI was seen during these moments.	Instruction was clearly designed to include the UDL principles. Additional supports were in place, so each learner had access and rigor.

Thank you for welcoming me into your room. Please see the comments section for additional details and specific feedback.

Comments:

© 2016 Elizabeth Stein

FIGURE A.3 CONT. Principal to Co-teachers Check-in

Class Learning Profile

Teacher: _____ Class/Grade Level: _____ School Year: _____

Network	Students' Strengths	Students' Needs	Students' Preferences/ Interests
Recognition (the "what" of learning)			
Strategic (the "how" of learning)			
Affect (the "why" of learning)			

© 2016 Elizabeth Stein

FIGURE A.4. Class Learning Profile Template

Class Learning Profile

Teacher: __Ms. L.__   Class/Grade Level: __4th__   School Year: _____

Network	Students' Strengths	Students' Needs	Students' Preferences/Interests
Recognition (the "what" of learning)	*Anthony* Reads with expression *Matthew* Enjoys opportunities to color or draw *Rachel* Participates with support *Teddy* Curious *Michael* Organized *Maria* Responds to commands when prompted or rewarded *Marissa* Enjoys participating in class and especially enjoys having her voice heard	*Anthony* Needs to slow down *Matthew* Comes to school tired; has low energy *Rachel* Decoding, word recognition *Teddy* Focuses on others, but needs to focus on himself *Michael* Impulsive; needs self-control *Maria* More independence, less prompting *Marissa* Needs to remain focused on herself, not others	*Anthony* Cars *Matthew* Drawing, dogs *Rachel* Animals, the movie *Frozen* *Teddy* Baseball, iPad *Michael* Video games *Maria* Predictable puzzles, snacks/foods *Marissa* Dolls/stuffed animals
Strategic (the "how" of learning)	*Anthony* Enthusiastic about computer or iPad work *Matthew* Enjoys illustrating *Rachel* Works best in small groups or 1:1 *Teddy* Average in spelling skills *Maria* Strengths in writing *Marissa* Likes to feel like she's helping others	*Anthony* Poor handwriting *Matthew* Rushes through work; wants others to believe he has finished first and/or convince others that he understands *Rachel* Needs to apply reading strategies; does not participate in large-group discussions *Teddy* Difficulty with written expression and multiple-step math problems *Maria* Restless/fidgety; has difficulty paying attention *Marissa* Speech impaired; fine motor delays; uses a pencil grip	

© 2016 Elizabeth Stein

FIGURE A.5. Class Learning Profile Sample

Class Learning Profile

Teacher: __Ms. L.__   Class/Grade Level: __4th__   School Year: _____

Network	Students' Strengths	Students' Needs	Students' Preferences/ Interests
Affect (the "why" of learning)	*Anthony* Willing to try new things; excited to begin new topics *Matthew* Encourages others; has family support *Rachel* Friendly, nurturing *Teddy* Responds very well to classroom behavior plan *Maria* High energy; tries hard to figure things out independently *Marissa* Enjoys being called on by teacher	*Anthony* Needs to increase stamina *Matthew* Easily confused by new concepts and directions; hard on himself, yet encourages others *Rachel* Does not have support at home *Teddy* Relies on others; does not complete work outside of school *Maria* High energy; easily discouraged *Marissa* Needs to accept constructive criticism; needs to be organized	

© 2016 Elizabeth Stein

FIGURE A.5 CONT. Class Learning Profile Sample

Students—How to Annotate a Text:

1. Chunk the reading: read the text in manageable sections.

2. Ask yourself: Do I understand the reading so far? Write your questions in the margins.

3. Underline key words and phrases in each section.

4. Jot key words in margins.

5. Summarize your understanding through your choice: sketch, create a chart, write a short summary, or discuss the key ideas with peers.

© 2016 Elizabeth Stein

FIGURE A.6. Student Application Cue Card

How to Annotate a Text

1. Look closely at the text—notice its structure, style, context, and imagery.
   - What does this section of reading make you think about?
   - What do you notice the author/poet does to help the readers understand what they are reading?

2. Notice what is said and how it is said. Underline, circle, and write in the margin. Make the text your own.

3. Jot down your thoughts in the margin by analyzing the text.
   - Write down what you notice.
   - Write down what you are thinking.
   - Paraphrase what you read in that section of the reading.

Active Reading Actions:

Visualize
Connect
Infer
Predict
Question
Paraphrase
Evaluate

Literary Devices to Notice:

Simile
Metaphor
Alliteration
Imagery
Personification
Tone (Author's Attitude)

© 2016 Elizabeth Stein

FIGURE A.7. Teacher Modeling Cue Card

Busting Co-teaching Barriers
Creating a Clear Path to Learning for All Learners
Names of the co-teachers: _____

Co-teaching Beliefs	Potential Barriers	Possible Solutions
What learning looks like in the co-taught classroom		
Classroom management		
Behavior management		
Role of each teacher		

Adapted by E. Stein, April 2015
Original Source: Rose, D. H., & Meyer, A. (2002). *Teaching every student in the digital age: Universal Design for Learning*. Alexandria, VA: ASCD.

© 2016 Elizabeth Stein

FIGURE A.8. Busting Co-teaching Barriers

Name:_____   Date:_____

Strengths-Based Check-in Reflection

1. What is one personal strength that you feel proud of?

2. Describe one way you are effective in communicating with others—for example, speaking, listening, writing, telling stories, telling jokes, and so forth.

3. What are your social strengths? Examples include leadership abilities, helpful to others, socializing, and showing empathy for others.

4. What are your emotional strengths? Examples include positive attitude most of the time, able to push through struggles, accepts guidance from others, and cares for other people.

5. Name one intellectual strength that you have—for example, musical, artistic, creative, math, science, nature, reading, and writing.

6. Name one physical strength that you have—for example, exercise, bike riding, skateboarding, and sports.

7. Tell us more! What other strengths do you have? What hobbies do you have?

© 2016 Elizabeth Stein

FIGURE A.9. Strengths-based Check-in Reflection

Dear Learners:

We are so excited to be your teachers this year! It is going to be an exciting year filled with curiosity and active learning. As a whole group, we create a community of learners where each voice matters! That means your voice is important as we create this comfortable learning environment.

So what do we mean by "your voice" anyway? Your voice is the thoughts you have quietly in your mind. It's the opinions, the connections, and the ideas that you think about as you observe your surroundings and participate in learning experiences. Your voice is unique to you—it is your ideas as you relate to the topics you will learn about this year.

Here are some ways you will strengthen your voice this year:

- You will begin to be more aware of what you think about the topics we discuss. That's right—your perspective is important!

- You will begin to be more comfortable sharing your thoughts with others. In addition to sharing your voice, you will listen to the voice of others. We will learn so much from one another.

- You may not always feel like sharing your thoughts out loud—and that's OK!

Here's what we, as your teachers, will do to guide you to connect more closely with your voice—and with learning in general:

1. We will provide options for you to make decisions. For example, sometimes you will have a choice to work with a partner or work on your own. We will also teach you strategies that will help you to take charge of your own learning. We will always be here to help you, but you will learn ways to motivate and set yourself up to be motivated to learn.

2. We will provide a variety of ways to present material to you. For example, sometimes we will use videos, images, texts, audio, and class discussions.

© 2016 Elizabeth Stein

FIGURE A.10. Letter to Learners

There will be times when you need to see what we're talking about. There will be other times when you need to listen, and yet other times when we will move around because that's the way you need to learn in those moments. So notice what works best for you—and tell us what you need!

3. We will provide many opportunities for you to collaborate with peers. You will learn strategies that work for you as you achieve your academic and personal goals. We will use a variety of tools, including technology, to communicate what we are learning. You will have a chance to speak, listen, write, sketch, and move about the room to express yourself!

We are looking forward to helping you to connect with who you are as a learner. This year will be an opportunity for you to not only value your voice, but also share it. We are looking forward to the process of you becoming your personal best this year!

Sincerely,

© 2016 Elizabeth Stein

FIGURE A.10 CONT. Letter to Learners

Dear Parents/Caregivers:

As you know, we are part of a powerful co-teaching team that values the learning experiences of each learner in the room. In addition to optimizing learning by sharing our individual teaching expertise, we value the individual strengths, abilities, and thoughts that your child brings to our community of learners. Our classroom environment invites each student to take part in a meaningful learning process. Each learner has the opportunity to listen, speak, read, write, and express his or her thoughts in a variety of ways. Students are comfortable to value their own voice and share within a risk-free learning environment.

One main component that allows us to be flexible with our teaching and learning experiences is by applying Universal Design for Learning (UDL) within our daily routine.

UDL is a framework that taps into what brain research shows us to be true about how people learn. We know that as we focus on creating an accessible curriculum, each student in the classroom will connect personally with the content and the process of learning. This UDL mindset empowers us to make the best instructional decisions possible for your children. Our UDL classroom naturally embeds the three principles that are essential for meaningful learning to take place.

1. **Multiple Means of Engagement:** Your child will experience learning as a purposeful, self-motivated learner. He or she will have opportunities to make choices, connect with peers through authentic collaborations and cooperative learning groups, and develop skills to strengthen his or her ability to self-regulate and motivate within a meaningful learning experience.

2. **Multiple Means of Representation:** Each week we will weave in a variety of ways to present information to our students. Your child will have the opportunity to perceive information in a variety of ways. For example, in addition to traditional text-based materials, we will be using digital tools to present

© 2016 Elizabeth Stein

FIGURE A.11. Letter to Parents and Caregivers

information to provide alternatives to visual and auditory information. Your child will be guided to connect what he or she already knows to new concepts students will be learning. By the end of the school year, your child will become a more resourceful and knowledgeable learner.

3. Multiple Means of Action & Expression: We include options for communication throughout the year to maximize your child's ability to express his or her understanding. Through purposeful goal setting, your child will co-create and apply the action steps needed to become a strategic thinker who monitors his or her effort and progress throughout the learning process.

For more information about UDL, please visit the Center for Applied Special Technology (CAST) at www.cast.org.

We are looking forward to a productive year of learning!

Sincerely,

© 2016 Elizabeth Stein

FIGURE A.11 CONT. Letter to Parents and Caregivers

Name: _____ Date: _____
Text: _____ Pages: _____
Topic: _____

Scan, Question, Read, Write

Scan:
- o Read the title
- o Introduction
- o Headings
- o Visuals
- o Captions
- o Bold print words

Question Words:

Who   What   Where
When Why   How

Question #1:
_____
_____

Write response #1:
_____
_____

Question #2:
_____
_____

Write response #2:
_____
_____

Question #3:
_____
_____

Write response #3:
_____
_____

© 2016 Elizabeth Stein

FIGURE A.12. Scan–Question–Read–Write Template

Question #4:
_____
_____

Write response #4:
_____
_____

Question #5:
_____
_____

Write response #5:
_____
_____

© 2016 Elizabeth Stein

FIGURE A.12 CONT. Scan-Question-Read-Write Template

UDL Learning Walk Information Sheet
Job-Embedded Professional Learning With Administrators

Overarching Goals:
- To co-create ICT and resource room learning environments that close students' personal achievement gaps through specially designed instruction
- To guide teachers to maintain high expectations for each learner in the room, resulting in learners who are knowledgeable and resourceful, strategic and goal directed, as well as purposeful and motivated
- To guide teachers to support learners who self-regulate and take charge of their learning through an intentionally designed instructional setting

In co-taught classrooms, answer the questions: *How is EACH teacher an invaluable addition to the instructional process? Where is the specially designed instruction?*

Process Goals:
1. The focus is on the learning process of the administrator as an observer. Administrators will deepen their understanding of Universal Design for Learning as we all strive to incorporate proactive differentiated instruction in all co-taught classrooms.
2. Educators will create equitable and meaningful learning experiences for all learners in inclusive settings (including the two teachers and administrators!).
    - Teachers will apply a UDL framework to pave the way for specially designed instruction, so every learner has the opportunity to personally connect with the content and process.
    - Administrators will notice and support effective co-teaching practices through the lens of UDL and SDI.

Why Learning Walks?
To engage administrators in meaningful learning about UDL and how it paves the way for specially designed instruction, proactive differentiated instruction, and consistent, equitable, meaningful learning experiences for all learners—including the two teachers in the room. Administrators play a key role in the process of implementing effective instruction in any classroom.

Key Elements for UDL Learning Walks
1. Create a shared understanding of purpose and process.
2. Align research-based strategies (that connect with UDL and SDI) with teachers' design that meet the needs of all learners.
3. Understand that the walk-throughs are a learning tool to deepen administrators' understanding of how UDL empowers learning for all learners and paves the way for specially designed instruction to take place in inclusive settings. This is not an evaluation of teachers' skills and instructional decisions.
4. Experience debriefs as discussions of practice—not judgments or evaluations of the observed teachers' practice or the administrators' knowledge and actions.
5. The process of UDL learning walks embraces a core UDL tenet—namely that we are all learners, learning from and with one another.

© 2016 Elizabeth Stein

FIGURE A.13. UDL Learning Walk Information Sheet

References

Armstrong, T. (2012). *Neurodiversity in the classroom: Strength-based strategies to help students with special needs succeed in school and life.* Association for Supervision and Curriculum Development.

Ashcroft, B., Griffiths, G., & Tiffin, H. (2013). *Post-colonial studies: The key concepts.* Routledge.

Bacharach, N., Heck, T. W., & Dahlberg, K. (2007). Co-teaching in higher education. *Journal of College Teaching & Learning, 4*(10).

Blachowicz, C. L. (1986). Making connections: Alternatives to the vocabulary notebook. *Journal of Reading, 29*(7), 643-649.

Blackwell, L. S., Trzesniewski, K. H., & Dweck, C. S. (2007). Implicit theories of intelligence predict achievement across an adolescent transition: A longitudinal study and an intervention. *Child Development, 78*(1), 246-263.

Carreker, S. (2004). *Developing metacognitive skills: Vocabulary and comprehension.* Neuhaus Education Center.

CAST (2018). Universal design for learning guidelines version 2.2 [graphic organizer]. Wakefield, MA: Author.

Collins, M., & Tamarkin, C. (1982). *Marva Collins' way.* J. P. Tarcher.

Cook, L., & Friend, M. (1995). Co-teaching: Guidelines for creating effective practices. *Focus on exceptional children, 28.*

Dweck, C. S. (2006). *Mindset: The new psychology of success.* Random House.

Dweck, C. S. (2007). Boosting achievement with messages that motivate. *Education Canada, 47*(2), 6-10.

Dweck, C. S. (2015). Carol Dweck revisits the growth mindset. *Education week, 35*(5), 20-24.

Ellis, E. S. (1997). Watering up the curriculum for adolescents with learning disabilities: Goals of the knowledge dimension. *Remedial and Special Education, 18,* 326-346.

Elmore, R. F. (2011). *I used to think . . . And now I think . . .* Harvard Education Press.

Ertmer, P. A., & Newby, T. J. (1996). The expert learner: Strategic, self-regulated, and reflective. *Instructional Science, 24*(1), 1-24.

Fischer, K. W. (1980). A theory of cognitive development: The control and construction of hierarchies of skills. *Psychological Review, 87*(6), 477.

Fischer, K. W., & Bidell, T. R. (2006). Dynamic development of action and thought. In R. M. Lerner & W. Damon (Eds.), *Handbook of child psychology: Theoretical models of human development* (pp. 313-399). John Wiley.

Freire, P. (2007). *Pedagogy of the oppressed.* Continuum. (Original work published 1970.)

Freire, P., & Macedo, D. (2005). *Literacy: Reading the word and the world.* Routledge.

Friend, M. (2015). Welcome to co-teaching 2.0. *Educational Leadership, 73*(4), 16–22.

Friend, M. (2016). Co-teaching as a special education service: Is classroom collaboration a sustainable practice? *Educational Practice and Reform, 2,* 1–12.

Friend, M., & Cook, L. (2007). *Co-teaching. Interactions: collaboration skills for professionals* (5th ed.). Pearson.

Gargiulo, R. M., & Metcalf, D. (2016). *Teaching in today's inclusive classrooms: A universal design for learning approach.* Cengage Learning.

Gately, S. E., & Gately, F. J., Jr. (2001). Understanding coteaching components. *Teaching exceptional children, 33*(4), 40–47.

Hall, T., Vue, G., Strangman, N., & Meyer, A. (2003). *Differentiated instruction and implications for UDL implementation.* National Center on Accessing the General Curriculum. (Links updated 2014). Retrieved August 17, 2022, from http://www.cast.org/products-services/resources/2003/ncac-differentiated-instruction-udl

Harvey, S., & Goudvis, A. (2007). *Strategies that work: Teaching comprehension for understanding and engagement.* Stenhouse Publishers.

Kalam, A., & Tiwari, A. (1999). *Wings of fire: An autobiography.* Universities Press (India).

Klingner, J. K., & Vaughn, S. (1999). Promoting reading comprehension, content learning, and English acquisition though Collaborative Strategic Reading (CSR). *The Reading Teacher, 52*(7), 738–747.

Lansdown, S. (1991). Increasing vocabulary knowledge using direct instruction, cooperative grouping, and reading in junior high school. *Illinois Reading Council Journal 19,* 15–21.

Meyer, A., Rose, D. H., & Gordon, D. T. (2014). *Universal design for learning: Theory and practice.* CAST Professional Publishing.

Palincsar, A. S., & Brown, A. L. (1984). Reciprocal teaching of comprehension-fostering and comprehension-monitoring activities. *Cognition and Instruction, 1*(2), 117–175.

Pintrich, P. R., & Zusho, A. (2002). The development of academic self-regulation: The role of cognitive and motivational factors. In *Development of achievement motivation* (pp. 249–284). Academic Press.

Reynolds, P. H. (2004). *Ish.* Walker Books.

Reynolds, P. H. (2009). *The north star.* Candlewick Press.

Robinson, K., & Aronica, L. (2014). *Finding your element: How to discover your talents and passions and transform your life.* Penguin.

Rose, D. H., & Meyer, A. (2002). *Teaching every student in the digital age: Universal design for learning.* Association for Supervision and Curriculum Development.

Rose, T. (2013). The myth of the average. TedX Sonoma County, June 19, 2013. www.youtube.com/watch?v=4eBmyttcfU4

Rose, T., Rouhani, P., & Fischer, K. W. (2013). The science of the individual. *Mind, Brain, and Education, 7*(3), 152–158.

Sabia, R. (2008, May/June). Universal Design for Learning and meaningful access to the curriculum. *TASH Connections*, 14–21.

Sams, A., & Bergmann, J. (2013). Flip your students' learning. *Educational Leadership, 70*(6), 16–20.

Shouse, E. (2005). Feeling, emotion, affect. *M/c journal, 8*(6).

Sousa, D. A., & Tomlinson, C. A. (2018). *Differentiation and the brain: How neuroscience supports the learner-friendly classroom* (2nd ed.). Solution Tree Press.

Stein, E. L. (2013). *Comprehension lessons for RTI grades 3–5: Assessments, intervention lessons, and management tips to help you reach and teach tier 2 students*. Scholastic Teaching Resources.

Stein, E. L. (2017). *Two teachers in the room: Strategies for co-teaching success*. Routledge.

Stein, E. L. (2021). *Co-creating a culture of belonging through the relational co-teaching framework: A critical, transformative auto ethnography* (doctoral dissertation, Molloy College).

Strichart, S. S., & Mangrum, C. T. (2002). *Teaching learning strategies and study skills to students with learning disabilities, attention deficit disorders, or special needs*. Allyn & Bacon.

Tomlinson, C. A. (1999). Mapping a route toward differentiated instruction. *Educational Leadership, 57*, 12–17.

Vacca, R. T., Vacca, J. A. L., Mraz, M. (2021). *Content area reading: Literacy and learning across the curriculum* (13th ed.). Pearson.

Vygotsky, L. S. (2012). *Thought and language*. MIT Press.

Vygotsky, L. S., & Cole, M. (1978). *Mind in society: Development of higher psychological processes*. Harvard University Press.

Weiss, M. P., Glaser, H., & Lloyd, J. W. (2020). An exploratory study of an instructional model for co-teaching. *Exceptionality*, 1–14.

Willingham, D. T. (2021). *Why don't students like school? A cognitive scientist answers questions about how the mind works and what it means for the classroom* (2nd ed.). Jossey-Bass.

Index

A
ABC analyses, 47
ability/disability spectrum, 9–10
    See also disabilities
accountable talk strategy, 142–143
action and expression
    examples, 91
    instruction planning, 81
    introducing students to, 96
    principle, 24–25, 26–27
    See also content-area strategies; peer collaboration strategies; student choice strategies
administrators
    as co-teaching supporters, 158–160
    in co-teaching university strategy, 176–178
    partnership approaches, 157–158
    principal to co-teachers template, 193–194
    in Story in Story scenarios, 168–174
    See also UDL learning walks
affective network
    with administrators, 160–161
    in Class Learning Profile, 62
    co-teaching examples, 30–31
    defined, 24, 25–26
alternative teaching, 50–51
assessments
    student choice, 123–124
    UDL approaches to, 35
Assignment Buddies, 122
assistance teaching model, 51

B
blackout notes, 138–139
brain
    as a muscle, 17–18
    learner variability research, 5–8

brain networks
    in Class Learning Profile, 62–63
    and co-teaching models, 29–31
    defined, 24
brainstorming
    breaks, 124–125
    exclusion strategy, 137–138
Busting Co-teaching Barriers template, 159, 189, 200

C
cards
    card pyramids, 134–136
    hint cards, 126–127
    Lansdown word cards, 143–144
check-ins
    co-teacher relationship, 92
    Colorful Conversation, 119
    principal to co-teachers template, 193–194
    Rose, Bud, Thorn, 105
    Stop, Jot, and Share, 69
    strategy reviews, 153
    strengths-based inventory, 65–66, 201
    "watering up" goals, 103–105
choice boards, 122–123
Class Learning Profile, 61–64, 195–197
clicks and clunks, 130
Clock Buddies, 122
co-teachers
    check-in tools, 69, 92, 105, 119, 153
    expertise, 39–40
    letter to principal sample, 191–192
    problem solving techniques, 178–179
    shared vision, 38
    See also general education teachers; special education teachers
co-teaching
    barriers, 44–46

213

co-teaching (continued)
   communication stages, 41
   and context, 5
   defined, 37–38
   key components, 38–39
   and learner variability, 7–8, 66–68
   mindsets, ix–xii, 18–20
   scenarios, 41–44, 86–90, 181–187
   with UDL Guidelines, 27–31
   with UDL principles, 91
co-teaching models
   alternative teaching, 50–51
   implementation, 51–54
   mapped to brain networks, 29–31
   "One Teaches, One Assists," 51
   "One Teaches, One Observes," 46–47
   parallel teaching, 48–49
   station teaching, 47–48
   team teaching, 49–50
co-teaching universe strategy, 174–179
collaborations
   modeling, 54
   as stage of co-teaching, 41
Collaborative Strategic Reading (CSR), 130–131
Colorful Conversation check-in, 119
communications
   stages, 40, 41
   transparent, 46
comprehension strategies, 138–139
concept organization strategies
   card pyramids, 134–136
   Keyword, Information, Memory (KIM), 140, 141
Connect, Collect, Correct strategy, 133–134
content-area strategies
   card pyramids, 134–136
   Collaborative Strategic Reading, 130–131
   concept circles, 136–137
   Connect, Collect, Correct, 133–134
   exclusion brainstorming, 137–138
   Fact, Question, Response, 132–133
   interactive notebooks, 131
   Keyword, Information, Memory clues, 140, 141
   Question–Answer–Detail, 88–89, 132
   reciprocal teaching, 129–130
   Scan, Question, Read, Write, 128–129, 206–207

contexts
   and dynamic skill theory, 5
   and expert learning, 14
   and learning styles, 68–69
Cornell notes, 87
corners exercise, 146–147
Crossley, Rosemary, xi
CSR (Collaborative Strategic Reading), 130–131
curricula
   assessment, 35
   goals, 32–33, 100–105
   materials, 33–34
   methods, 34–35

D

deficit model, 8–10, 77–78
differentiated instruction
   in Planning Prompts, 112
   and UDL, 75–80
digital materials, 33
disabilities
   ability/disability spectrum, 9–10
   and instruction planning, 77–78
   learned helplessness, 99
discussion strategies
   accountable talk, 142–143
   learning links, 150–151
   move into corners, 146–147
   text on text, 144–146
Dweck, Carol, 17, 18
dynamic skill theory, 5

E

EdWordle, 137
Ellis, Edwin, 100, 103
Elmore, Richard F., 184
emotions, 6
engagement
   examples, 91
   instruction planning, 81
   introducing students to, 96
   principle, 25, 26
   supporting, 97–99
   See also content-area strategies; peer collaboration strategies; student choice strategies
EQ (essential question), 112
exclusion brainstorming, 137–138

expert learners
    characteristics, 16, 63–64
    cultivating, 13–15

F

Fact, Question, Response (FQR) strategy, 132–133
Fischer, Kurt, 5
flextime periods, 127–128
flipped learning, 114–118
formative assessments, 35
Friend, Marilyn, 37, 38, 46, 72

G

gallery walks, 149–150
general education teachers
    in co-teaching classrooms, 39, 45–46
    in Story in Story scenarios, 168–174
goals, 32–33
growth mindsets, 17–18
guided notes, 116–117

H

hint cards, 126–127

I

"I Do, We Do, You Do" model, 55, 84
inclusion vs. co-teaching, 38
Individualized Education Plans (IEPs), 32, 72
Individuals with Disabilities Education Act (IDEA), 8–9
instruction design
    co-teaching model selection, 52–54
    with UDL, 27–31
    See also specially designed instruction (SDI)
instruction planning, 3–4, 80–83
    See also differentiated instruction; specially designed instruction (SDI)
instructional goals, 32
interactive notebooks, 131
Ish (Reynolds), 97

K

Kalah, Abdul, on positive learning, 96
Keyword, Information, Memory (KIM) strategy, 140, 141

L

language, influence of, 18, 76
Lansdown word cards, 143–144
learned helplessness, 99
learner variability
    vs. deficit model, 8–10
    defined, 4–5
    and expectations, 99–102
    and learning styles, 68–69
    planning for, 24–27, 66–68
    theory, 5–6
    and UDL, 7–8
learners
    abilities and disabilities, 8–10
    brain networks, 24
    expert, 13–16, 63–64
    letter to learners sample, 202–203
    See also learner variability; students
learning links exercise, 150–151
learning process
    mindsets for, 18
    modeling, 50
    motivation, 13–14
    student self-monitoring, 98–99
learning styles, 68–69
lesson plans and planning
    Planning Prompts, 110–114
    with UDL principles, 24–25, 109–110
"Let's Do This!" approach, 157–158
line-ups exercise, 151–152

M

materials, 33–34
method approaches, 34–35
Meyer, Anne, 6, 9, 24, 27, 31, 61
    Universal Design for Learning: Theory and Practice, 24
mindsets
    administrator, 160
    co-teaching, ix–xii, 18–20
    growth, 17
    UDL, 10, 181

N

North Star, The (Reynolds), 97
notes
    Connect, Collect, Correct strategy, 133–134
    Cornell notes, 87

notes *(continued)*
  Fact, Question, Response strategy, 132–133
  guided, 116–117
  interactive notebooks, 131
  Question–Answer–Detail strategy, 132

O

observation
  administrator walk-throughs, 159–160
  as co-teaching model, 46–47
  See also UDL learning walks
"One Teaches, One Assists" model, 51
"One Teaches, One Observes" model, 46–47

P

Padlet, 151
parallel teaching, 48–49
parents, sample letter to, 204–205
peer collaboration strategies, 140, 142–152
  accountable talk, 142–143
  gallery walks, 149–150
  Lansdown word cards, 143–144
  learning links, 150–151
  line-ups, 151–152
  move into corners, 146–147
  paraphrasing tickets, 149
  peer-to-peer think-aloud, 148
  "points to ponder," 147
  text on text, 144–146
peer-to-peer think-aloud strategy, 148
picture books, 97
Planning Prompts, 110–118
"points to ponder" strategy, 147

Q

Question–Answer–Detail (QAD) strategy, 88–89, 132
Quizlet, 116

R

reading strategies
  blackout notes, 138–139
  Collaborative Strategic Reading, 130–131
  reciprocal teaching, 129–130
  Scan, Question, Read, Write, 128–129, 206–207
reciprocal teaching, 129–130
recognition network
  in Class Learning Profile, 62
  co-teaching examples, 29–31
  defined, 24
representation
  examples, 91
  instruction planning, 81
  introducing students to, 96
  principle, 24–25, 27
  See also content-area strategies; peer collaboration strategies; student choice strategies
research skill development, 125–126
Reynolds, Peter, 97
Robinson, Sir Ken, 83
Rose, Bud, Thorn check-in, 105
Rose, David, 5, 9, 24, 27, 61

S

Sabia, Ricki, 33, 34
scaffolds and scaffolding
  examples, 80–83, 86–90
  tips for effective, 85
  "watering up the curriculum," 100–105
  and zone of proximal development, 83–84
Scan, Question, Read, Write (SQRW), 128–129, 206–207
SDI. *See* specially designed instruction (SDI)
self-regulation
  development, 98–99
  in expert learners, 14, 16
  supports, 34, 126, 144, 166
shared vision, 38, 190
skills theory, 5
"Sounds Great!" approach, 158
special education, 8–10
special education teachers
  in co-teaching classrooms, 39, 73–74
  in Story in Story scenarios, 168–174
specially designed instruction (SDI)
  and learning variability, 74–75
  overview, 72–74
SQRW (Scan, Question, Read, Write), 128–129, 206–207
station teaching, 47–48
Stop, Jot, and Share check-in, 69
Story in Story (SiS) approach, 168–174
strategic network
  in Class Learning Profile, 62
  co-teaching examples, 29–31
  defined, 24–25

strengths-based inventory, 65–66, 201
student application cue card, 198
student choice strategies, 122–128
    assessments, 123–124
    brainstorming breaks, 124–125
    choice boards, 122–123
    flextime, 127–128
    hint cards, 126–127
    inquiry teams, 125–126
    seating choice, 122
students
    introduction to UDL, 96
    self-regulation, 98–99
    in Story in Story scenario, 172–174
    strengths-based inventories, 65–66, 201
    See also learners
systematic variability, 4–5
    See also learner variability

T

taking turns trap, 186
teacher modeling cue card, 199
teacher-student interviews, 66
teachers
    preservice, 110
    See also general education teachers; special education teachers
team teaching, 49–50
templates
    Class Learning Profile, 195–197
    letter to learners sample, 202–203
    letter to parents and caregivers sample, 204–205
    letter to principal sample, 191–192
    principal to co-teachers check-in, 193–194
    Scan, Question, Read, Write, 206–207
    shared vision planning, 190
    strengths-based check-in reflection, 201
    student application cue card, 198
    teacher modeling cue card, 199
    UDL Learning Walk, 208
text on text exercise, 144–146
think-on-your-feet strategies, 151–152

U

UDL (Universal Design Learning)
    defined, xiii
    and differentiated instruction, 75–80
    goals under, 32–33
    mindset, x, 10, 181
    supporting high expectations, 100–102
UDL action steps, 66–68
UDL Guidelines
    and brain networks, 29–31
    on expert learners, 15–16, 63–64
UDL learning walks, 161–168, 189, 208
    classroom visit, 162–165
    debrief, 165
    facilitator responsibilities, 168
    preparation, 161–162
    sample notes, 166–167
    template, 189, 208
UDL principles
    co-teaching suggestions, 91
    and flexible lesson planning, 24–27
    introducing students to, 96
    and learner variability, 7
Universal Design for Learning: Theory and Practice (Meyer), 24

V

vision. *See* shared vision
vocabulary strategies
    concept circles, 136–137
    Keyword, Information, Memory, 140, 141
    Lansdown word cards, 143–144
    paraphrasing tickets, 149
Vygotsky, Lev, 54–55, 83–84

W

"watering up the curriculum," 100–105
Willingham, Daniel, 68
word clouds, 137
word lists, in co-teaching universe, 174–179
workshop structures, 54–56

Y

"You are the Teacher," 116

Z

zone of actual development (ZAD), 54
zone of proximal development (ZPD), 54, 83–84

Acknowledgments

Readers, here we are! The publication of this second edition exists with gratitude to all the dedicated educators whose interest in the first edition created the opportunity for this expanded and updated version. The book *Elevating Co-teaching With Universal Design for Learning, Revised and Expanded*, celebrates individuals as evolving, collaborative learners. The first edition was written as the result of a personal journal I kept as I grappled with creating meaningful co-teaching experiences when I was in the classroom full-time. And it certainly was not always easy. I am grateful for all my co-teaching partners over time—yes, every one of them. It is easy to feel grateful when things are going well. Yet, my gratitude extends even during the most challenging co-teaching situations.

The UDL framework was always a reassuring structure that became my mindset as I strived to design accessible and meaningful learning experiences. UDL became the cushion I fell back on whenever discouragement set in as I attempted to apply co-teaching practices. This second edition builds upon the history of the first with an emphasis on how grateful I am to everyone who empowered me as an evolving learner through the years. This expanded edition is evidence of that. I never imagined the first edition being like the golden ticket that invited me into so many schools and classrooms near and far—I am grateful to all the students, teachers, administrators, and parents for our ongoing connections and collaborations.

Thank you, Marilyn Friend. Your work has been such a strong part of guiding and grounding my clear focus on expanding possibilities in co-taught, inclusive classrooms since my first teaching experience in 1990 and throughout the years since! Your work and wisdom have grounded my knowledge and my ability to act when advocating for the active participation of special education teachers alongside their general education teaching partners. I am honored to have this opportunity to share my gratitude with you for the influence your work has on my own.

I am grateful to David Rose and Anne Meyer for their vision in applying universal design in architecture to education. As co-founders of UDL, you have co-created an ever-evolving process that invites every educator, administrator, and stakeholder to expand possibilities for every learner in any classroom.

David Gordon, where do I even begin to thank you? As my editor of the first edition and now the second edition, you have shaped my thinking and validated the ways I personally view and live the UDL experience. Your calm, clear way of thinking, communicating, and being during our email conversations and our video-call planning sessions were always a welcome part of this publication process.

Thank you, Billie Fitzpatrick, for your guidance in designing the structure of the first edition and remaining a part of the team for this second edition. Allison Posey, your kind, specific feedback was always a welcome support as I worked through the writing process for this second edition. Rachel Monaghan, thank you for your keen eye and caring commitment in creating a smooth and timely copyediting stage. I feel honored to be associated with CAST Professional Publishing, and I am grateful to every member of my publishing team.

Thank you to my family—you know you come first, foremost, and forever. To all the individuals who have influenced the making of this second edition, please know that my expression of gratitude moves beyond words on a page—they are words that spring into action, in empowering ways, every day.

About the Author

ELIZABETH STEIN, EdD, has been a special education teacher, instructional coach, and educational consultant for more than 30 years, specializing in universal design for learning (UDL) and co-taught inclusive practices. She is an adjunct professor at Stony Brook University, New York. Elizabeth is a renewed National Board Certified Teacher (NBCT) in literacy and the author of *Two Teachers in the Room: Strategies for Co-teaching Success* (Routledge, 2017) and other publications.

More from CAST Professional Publishing

UDL Now! A Teacher's Guide to Applying Universal Design for Learning, Third Edition

By Katie Novak, with a foreword by George Couros

"Katie Novak's well-articulated know-how, about how to put UDL into practice, has helped many thousands of educators . . . She can describe what she does without evaporating the awe, the joy, or the sublimity of what great teaching is really like."

—DAVID H. ROSE, co-founder of CAST

ISBN 978-1-930583-82-5 (Print)
ISBN 978-1-930583-83-2 (ePub)
196 PAGES | © 2022

Transform Your Teaching with Universal Design for Learning: Six Steps to Jumpstart Your Practice

By Jennifer L. Pusateri

"Putting UDL into practice can be daunting for teachers who are just starting out. Jennifer L. Pusateri puts them at ease as she suggests step-by-step strategies to transform our teaching with this powerful framework."

—ANDRATESHA FRITZGERALD, founder of Building Blocks of Brilliance LLC

ISBN 978-1-930583-95-5 (Print)
ISBN 978-1-930583-94-8 (ePub)
224 PAGES | © 2022

Unlearning: Changing Your Beliefs and Your Classroom with UDL

By Allison Posey and Katie Novak

"[The authors] not only take on system reform but ask us to examine our embedded beliefs of what learning is. They encourage readers to be bold and assertive in examining their assumptions, by creating space for self-discovery and sharing insights from their own journeys."

—BRYAN DEAN, UDL Innovation Specialist

ISBN 978-1-930583-44-3 (Print)
ISBN 978-1-930583-47-4 (ePub)
128 PAGES | © 2020

For more information, visit **www.castpublishing.org** or wherever books are sold. For bulk orders, email **publishing@cast.org**.

More from CAST Professional Publishing

Antiracism and Universal Design for Learning: Building Expressways to Success

By Andratesha Fritzgerald, with a foreword by Samaria Rice

"Fritzgerald offers very practical suggestions for making inclusion, antiracism, and the acceptance of differences the first and most important step in lesson planning . . . This book gives me hope that, in education, we can begin to eliminate the violence of academic and social prejudice that kills the spirit of our babies and belittles the needs and experiences of people of color."

—SAMARIA RICE, founder and CEO of the Tamir Rice Foundation

ISBN 978-1-930583-70-2 (Print)
ISBN 978-1-930583-71-9 (ePub)
192 PAGES | © 2020

Supercharge Your Professional Learning: 40 Practical Strategies that Improve Adult Learning

By Kasia M. Derbiszewska and T. Nicole Tucker-Smith

"Drawing on their passion for staff development and deep knowledge of best practices, including UDL, the authors offer a power-packed guide to professional learning that is both rewarding and fun."

—JENNIFER LEVINE, Chief Academic Officer, CAST

ISBN 978-1-930583-74-0 (Print)
ISBN 978-1-930583-39-9 (ePub)
126 PAGES | © 2020

Elli: A Day in the Life of a Kid with ADHD

By Ari H.G. Yates

"My name is Elli, and this book is about me! I'm 9 years old and I have ADHD. In this book, I want to explain what it's like having ADHD, the bad and the good. Maybe another kid can read this book and realize that many others have ADHD, and even though it can be difficult, you can still accomplish a lot of cool things . . . Especially if you understand your ADHD better!"

—A message from Elli, who inspired the book

ISBN 978-1-930583-90-0 (Print)
ISBN 978-1-930583-91-7 (ePub)
40 PAGES | © 2021

For more information, visit **www.castpublishing.org** or wherever books are sold. For bulk orders, email **publishing@cast.org**.

MORE FROM CAST

CAST is a nonprofit education research and development organization that created the Universal Design for Learning framework and UDL Guidelines. Our mission is to transform education design and practice until learning has no limits.

CAST supports learners and educators at every level through a variety of offerings:

- Innovative professional development
- Accessibility and inclusive technology resources
- Research, design, and development of inclusive and effective solutions
- Credentials for Universal Design for Learning
- And much more

Visit *www.cast.org* to learn more.

CAST | Until learning has no limits®